FOSSIL RIDGE PUBLIC LIBRARY DISTRICT

3 2186 00079 8032

W9-CBR-400

Fossil Ridge Public Library District
386 Kennedy Road
Braidwood, Illinois 60408

GAYLORD

Victoria

AND HER TIMES

Jean-Loup Chiflet
Alain Beaulet

A Henry Holt Reference Book

Henry Holt and Company

New York

FOSSIL RIDGE PUBLIC LIBRARY DISTRICT
Braidwood, IL 60408

A PICTURE IS WORTH A THOUSAND WORDS

Xun Zi (313-238 B.C.)

A Henry Holt Reference Book
Henry Holt and Company, Inc.
Publishers since 1866
115 West 18th Street
New York, New York 10011

Henry Holt® is a registered trademark
of Henry Holt and Company, Inc.

Copyright © 1996 by Editions Mango
American English translation copyright © 1996 by
Henry Holt and Company, Inc.
All rights reserved.
Published in Canada by Fitzhenry & Whiteside Ltd.,
195 Allstate Parkway, Markham, Ontario L3R 4T8.

Library of Congress Cataloging-in-Publication Data
Chiflet, Jean-Loup.
[Victoria et son temps. English]
Victoria and her times/Jean-Loup Chiflet and Alain
Beaulet.
p. cm.

—(A Henry Holt reference book) (W5)
Includes bibliographical references (p.) and index.
Summary: Examines how new inventions, scientific
advances, and imperialism changed life in England during
the reign of Queen Victoria.
1. Great Britain—History—Victoria, 1837-1901—Juvenile
literature. 2. Great Britain—Civilization—19th century—
Juvenile literature. 3. Victoria, Queen of Great Britain,
1819-1901—Juvenile literature. [1. Great Britain—
History—Victoria, 1837-1901. 2. Great Britain—
Civilization—19th century. 3. Victoria, Queen of Great
Britain, 1819-1901.] I. Beaulet, Alain. II. Title. III. Series.
IV. Series: W5 (who, what, where, when, and why) series.
DA550.C55   1996   96-28394
941.081—dc20   CIP
                                                          AC

ISBN 0-8050-5084-1

Henry Holt books are available for special
promotions and premiums.
For details contact: Director, Special Markets.

Originally published in France in 1996 by
Editions Mango under the title *Victoria et son temps*.

First published in the United States in 1996
by Henry Holt and Company, Inc.

First American Edition—1996

Idea and series by Dominique Gaussen
American English translation by George Wen
Typesetting by Jay Hyams and
Christopher Hyams Hart
Printed in Italy by G. Canale & C. S.p.A. - Borgaro T.se - TURIN
All first editions are printed on acid-free paper. ∞
1 2 3 4 5 6 7 8 9 10

England was the first modern state worthy of the name and served as a model for many other countries. It achieved this status thanks in part to the leadership of two women—Elizabeth I and Queen Victoria—who saw the country through its most glorious times.

Before those extraordinary women appeared on the scene, several men made an impact on this country as well. In 55 B.C. Julius Caesar crossed the English Channel with two legions and landed in the British Isles, which he called Britannia. Roman rule lasted there four centuries. Then, during the period of the fall of Rome, the legionnaires were withdrawn so they could be used to defend other parts of the empire from barbarian attacks. Britain was abandoned.

In the four centuries that followed, the country was occupied successively by the Picts and Scots from the north and three Germanic tribes from the European continent: the Jutes, Saxons, and Angles (*England* means "land of the Angles"). A number of Britons fled to Gaul during this time and settled in the area that later took the name of Brittany. In 827 Egbert, king of Wessex, succeeded in uniting the patchwork of kingdoms into what later became modern England— Egbert is often called the first king of England.

Shortly after, the Danes launched major invasions of England. King Alfred the Great led the resistance against the invaders and in 878 defeated them at the Battle of Edington, thus halting their advance in England for a time. The Danes made renewed attacks on England from 994 until 1016, when Canute succeeded in defeating the English. Canute reigned as king of England and ruled wisely. His two descendants ruled England until 1042.

Edward the Confessor succeeded the last Danish king and thus restored Anglo-Saxon rule to England. At his death, Edward named Harold his successor, even though his cousin, William of Normandy, had legitimate claims to the throne. William decided to fight for his claim and invaded England with an army of 50,000 men. He defeated the English in 1066 at the Battle of Hastings, an event that was immortalized by the celebrated Bayeux tapestry.

On Christmas Day, William I was crowned king of England. For future generations he became known as William the Conqueror, and he was one of the greatest monarchs among the thirty-four kings and queens of England who preceded Victoria to the throne. Queen Victoria held the record for longevity of rule, reigning for sixty-four years, from 1837 to 1901. Her ancestor Elizabeth I didn't do so badly herself: she reigned for forty-five years (1558-1603). After William the Conqueror, the English kings found themselves lords of a number of French provinces, and because of the type of government of the day, they had to pay allegiance to the kings of France or lose their possessions. This situation did little to please Edward III, and he sought to claim the French crown for himself—after all, he was the grandson of the French king Philip IV. And so began, in 1337, the Hundred Years War between England and France. The English were victorious at the battles of Crécy, Poitiers, and then Agincourt in 1415, where France's best knights were defeated. It is not surprising that the

ARE TRUMP

French suffered the losses they did since they were being led by a king who was becoming increasingly insane. By 1492 Henry V of England controlled practically all of France north of the Loire River and had Orléans under siege. French king Charles VI had been forced to recognize Henry as regent and heir to the throne of France, disinheriting his own son, the dauphin. French fortunes were reversed, however, when Joan of Arc lifted the siege of Orléans and saw the dauphin crowned as Charles VII at Rheims. Her capture and execution did not end the string of victories for the French, and by 1453 the English had lost everything except Calais, which they managed to retain until 1558. That war over, another took its place, this time the civil war known as the Wars of the Roses, which pitted the noble house of Lancaster (whose badge was a red rose) against the house of York (whose badge was a white rose). Henry VII of the house of Lancaster brought an end to the wars and founded the Tudor dynasty. His son, Henry VIII, created his own church—the Church of England—when he was unable to obtain permission from the pope to divorce his first wife. Henry VIII's daughter Elizabeth I inherited the throne in 1558 at the age of twenty-five. Her rule was marked by England's rise as a commercial, colonial, and naval power. The Armada assembled by Philip II of Spain proved no match for the English fleet, and its defeat broke the power of Spain and strengthened England's national pride. The Elizabethan Age also saw the cultural flowering of England, including William Shakespeare. During her reign, Elizabeth upheld the Church of England, and this single-mindedness had the effect of galvanizing the divergent religious factions into war. The English civil war—also known as the Puritan Revolution—was a conflict between Charles I and a large body of his subjects, the Puritans, that ended with the defeat and execution of the king and the establishment of a republican Commonwealth. Oliver Cromwell was named lord protector of England in 1653, and after his death, Charles II, the son of Charles I, was restored to the throne by Parliament. In the eighteenth century, England played a leading role in the wars of succession that rocked Europe. With the signing of the Peace of Utrecht in 1713, which ended the War of the Spanish Succession, England was given the islands of Minorca and Gilbraltar and received Acadia, Newfoundland, and much of the Hudson Bay region from the French. The Treaty of Paris of 1763 gave England Canada, India, and a number of islands in the West Indies and marked Britain's rise as the dominant colonial power. The American Revolution, which began in 1775, ended with another Treaty of Paris, in 1783, whereby Great Britain formally acknowledged the independence of the Thirteen Colonies as the United States. At the beginning of the nineteenth century, Britain took an active part in the wars against Napoleon. Nelson defeated the combined fleets of France and Spain at Trafalgar, and Wellington's victory at Waterloo in 1815 spelled the end of the war. George III had been sitting on the throne of England since 1760. Born in 1738, he was the first king of the German house of Hanover who spoke English without an accent. His reign witnessed a great expansion of empire and trade, the beginning of the Industrial Revolution, and a flowering of arts and letters. He wasn't such a bad king, but he lost his sanity in 1810, and with it his power. What was going to happen now? Was England in trouble? Who was going to deal the cards? And who was going to lay his cards on the table? Was it going to be a simple game of poker or a free-for-all? Who would be the winner? Ace, king, jack, or queen?

I remember that on the day of my christening my uncle Elizabeth. In the end, the name chosen was Alexandrina remember that my father, the duke of Kent, died of I sometimes got so mad that I stamped my foot on the my childhood. I remember that German was the first I said "Goot mornink" instead of "Good morning." I pulling me in my cart bolted and I was saved by a brave a very beautiful doll collection that I didn't want my friend hated playing the piano but loved painting. I remember that Fraülein Lehzen. I remember that on a visit to my aunt everyone to let me clean the windows because it was forbidden palace. I remember that my uncle George IV gave me a remember that my mother, the duchess of Kent, never allowed conversation with anyone without her being present. I official governess, the duchess of Northumberland, was of my beloved Lehzen. I remember that I was terrified of the because of the wigs they wore. I remember that I had a

I REMEMBER

wanted me to be called Georgina, while my father insisted on Victoria. I remember I had blond hair and blue eyes. I pneumonia when I was barely a year old. I remember that ground. I remember that I slept with my mother all through language I spoke and that I made my uncles laugh whenever remember that when I was three years old the pony that was Irish soldier. I remember that I had Jane to touch. I remember that I I adored my governess Adelaide's I begged for me to do it at home in the donkey as a present. I me to have a minute's remember that my exceedingly jealous church bishops dancing teacher, a

GET SET, GO!

In 1810, at the age of seventy-two, George III is declared insane. He is the father of fifteen children, twelve of whom, aging princes and princesses, are still alive. His eldest son, the prince of Wales, has only one child, a daughter named Charlotte. She marries the German prince Leopold of Saxe-Coburg, and then, on November 6, 1817, at age twenty-one, she dies with her stillborn son after fifty hours in labor. Since she was heiress to the throne after her father, her death creates a break in the British royal succession. Who's next in line?

The prince of Wales hates his wife so much that he vows to never have children with her again. The duke of York is married to the princess royal of Prussia, but she prefers the company of her dogs, monkeys, and parrots to her husband's; they remain childless. The duke of Clarence has had ten children with his longtime mistress, the well-known actress Mrs. Dorothy Jordan, but they are all, of course, illegitimate. The amazingly ugly and unpopular duke of Cumberland has bravely wed a twice-widowed German princess rumored to have murdered her previous husbands; they are childless. The duke of Sussex married Lady Augusta Murray and then, after her death, Lady Cecilia Buggin; since neither match received the consent of the king, both are void, and the duke's son and daughter by Lady Augusta Murray are not in the line of succession to the throne. The duke of Cambridge, George III's youngest son, spends most of his time in the family's German kingdom of Hanover; he wears a blond wig, whiles away many hours playing the violin, and shows no interest in fathering children. All five of the king's daughters are spinsters or childless.

That leaves the fifty-year-old duke of Kent. He promptly answers the call of dynastic duty by leaving his mistress of twenty-seven years, Madame de St. Laurent, to marry Mary Louisa Victoria of Saxe-Coburg, princess of Meiningen, widow of Prince Emich Karl of Meiningen, and, more important, sister of Leopold, his late niece Charlotte's husband.

Then the duke of Clarence decides he doesn't want to be left out of the race for the throne. He renounces Mrs. Jordan to marry the more suitable Princess Adelaide of Saxe-Meiningen.

Victoria, daughter of the duke of Kent, is born on May 24, 1819. She is fifth in succession, so her chances of sitting on the throne seem remote. George III, her grandfather, is still king. After him in line of succession are her uncles the prince of Wales and the dukes of York and Clarence and finally her own father. The duke of Kent is fifty-two years old, strong and healthy, his wife is only thirty-three, so the chances of a male heir are good. Apart from this, the duchess of Clarence, whose infant daughter died two months before Victoria was born, might have other children. (In fact the duchess bears one more daughter, who dies twelve weeks later, and stillborn twins.)

But within eight weeks of her birth baby Victoria moves two degrees closer to the throne. On January 23, 1820, her father dies of inflammation of the lungs, the result of a bad cold. Six days later her grandfather the aged George III is also dead. The death of the duke of York in 1827 puts the duke of Clarence next in line to the throne. When George IV dies in 1830, the duke succeeds him as William IV. His reign lasts only seven years. His niece, Victoria, is only eighteen when she takes her place on the throne of England. For her, it has been an amazing process of elimination!

9

THE FORTUNE-TELLER

In 1802 the duke of Kent is sent to Gibraltar to restore order to an unruly garrison. A fanatic about discipline, he carries out his job with such severity that a serious mutiny breaks out, and he's recalled to London.

While still in Gibraltar, however, the duke somehow meets a gypsy fortuneteller who predicts that he will father a great queen. Years later, while he is serving in Germany and the duchess is expecting their first child, the duke remembers what the gypsy told him. Not superstitious by nature, the duke nonetheless decides that this child must, at whatever cost, be born in England, where she will fulfill her glorious destiny. Preparations are made to return to England, and it is there on English soil that the future queen first opens her eyes, on May 24, 1819.

Let's imagine what else the gypsy fortuneteller might have said had the duke pressed her to look deeper into her crystal ball.

"I see a very young girl in a great cathedral. She is acclaimed by crowds of people. I see an elderly statesman who takes the young queen under his wing. She confides in him and shows him affection. I see young German cousins visiting her. I see a very beautiful love story unfolding. I see many children. I see a country in the throes of political and industrial upheaval. I see men and women of extraordinary valor who will sacrifice their lives to fight against misery and injustice. I see savage wars, I see forests, lances, masks, turbans, elephants, tigers, I see a cruel jungle, I see a sun that never sets on the young girl's realm. I see very young children who suffer and who work, and I see people dancing. I see a great palace in glass like an immense window where amazing objects are displayed and admired by throngs of people. I see great misfortune. I see the end of the love story, I see a widow who is inconsolable, I see great red-brick houses, crinoline dresses, horses, coaches, uniforms. I see danger, I see assassination attempts. I see hate and I also see longstanding enemies coming together in a spirit of friendship. I see millions of men fighting for her glory, I see monuments, mountains, rivers, and lakes that bear her name. I see people dying of starvation on an island close by, very close by. I see an entire people at her feet. I see more misery. I see machines that run on steam, on coal. I see boats. I see children from her children who wear crowns. I see a tiny woman who has become a great empress."

AN INVENTORY OF THE HOUSE OF ENGLAND

When the prime minister, Lord Melbourne, hands over the keys of the House of England to young Victoria in 1837, the country is not in great shape. On the plus side, of course, Britain has the world's most powerful navy ❶ and its overseas empire is expanding all over the place ❷, but on the negative side the country has an enormous budgetary deficit ❸ and is rife with dissent from a group of working-class social and political reformers called Chartists, who are prepared to use violence to achieve their goals ❹. The largely Catholic Ireland ❺ is in the throes of a full-blown crisis. Good news, though: British coal production ❻ has more than doubled since 1800, from 11 to 23 million tons. The country is still in the hands of the landed gentry ❼. At the close of the Congress of Vienna, Britain is the foremost power in the world ❽ and is little inclined to seek out alliances of any kind.

A choice of leather, linen, and silk gloves.

Straw hat in a burnished bronze satin finish with a pastel blue calotte.

Black velvet-lined calotte with an egret feather held in place by a rhinestone brooch.

Long, red wool shawl with cream-colored lining over a batiste skirt tied over a muslin bodice.

Laced-trimmed linen undergarments.

REAL SECRETS

Silk stockings with hidden
stitches, reinforced heels, and
floral-pattern garters.

Flowered sateen and
flanette bathing
costume, threaded in
lace with ribbons, with
a generous neckline.

Tailored outfit
with jacket and
jabot in puffed
taffeta with
draping over the
skirt.

Double lacing
whale-bone corset
with Valenciennes
lace insertions.

Beige taffeta dress trimmed with embroideries
in cashmere, a slightly loose-fitting bodice
in seersucker with matching
satin.

Linen corset
overgarment
trimmed with lace
and silk ribbons.

Love,
the silent stream,
is found
Beneath the willows
lurking,
The deeper that it has
no sound
To tell its ceaseless
working.

LOVE STORY

Victoria is well aware that she's the world's most prized catch. She gets plenty of marriage proposals, but no one catches her fancy, and she isn't in any particular hurry. But her darling uncle King Leopold I of Belgium is a schemer. To him, nothing could be more perfect than to unite the young queen with one of his two nephews, the sons of his brother Prince Ernest of Saxe-Coburg. After all, they're both well brought up guys, each with a superb education. Of the two, Leopold is partial to Albert. The young prince has everything going for him—he's tall, handsome, smart, and full of life. On May 18, 1836, Victoria meets her cousins for the first time in London. During their stay Victoria has eyes only for Albert, and though she wants more time to ponder something as serious as marriage (she figures another four years ought to do the trick!) she quickly invites Albert back to London for another visit. Her mind is made up. But Albert has reservations. "V. is said to be incredibly stubborn," the young prince writes to a friend. "And her extreme obstinacy is at war with her good nature; she delights in court ceremonies, etiquette, and trivial formalities. She is said to take not the slightest pleasure in nature, to enjoy sitting up late at night and sleeping late into the day." All this is true, but when Victoria pops the question, the prince throws everything to the winds and accepts her proposal. (The queen has to pluck up the courage to propose—Prince Albert's lower rank makes it impossible for him to speak first.) The wedding takes place on February 10, 1840, in the chapel of St. James's Palace. That morning the queen sends a note by hand to her fiance: *How are you today, and have you slept well? I have rested very well, and feel very comfortable today. What weather! I believe, however, the rain will cease.*

Send one word when you, my most dearly loved bridegroom, will be ready.

Thy ever-faithful, Victoria R.

The next day, snatching a little time from worshiping her new husband, she pours out her happiness to her uncle King Leopold:

I don't think it possible for anyone in the world to be happier, or as happy as I am. He is an angel, and his kindness and affection toward me is really touching. To look in those dear eyes, and that dear sunny face, is enough to make me adore him. What I can do to make him happy will be my greatest delight.

Thanks to Albert, Victoria has finally found peace and stability. Their marriage brings her happiness she has never known before. In their first years together, Albert does not attend the queen's meetings with her ministers. Later on, there's not a single meeting he doesn't attend, always keeping abreast of everything that's going on. He has a passion for work and takes on enormous tasks in order to lighten his wife's burdens. It is for him that the queen creates the title prince consort. Their honeymoon lasts more than two decades.

A PRINCELY RESUME

Last name: Saxe-Coburg-Gotha

First name: Albert

Date of birth: August 26, 1819

Place of birth: Rosenau, Coburg

Marital status: Married with 9 children

Places of residence: Windsor and Balmoral castles and Osborne House, Great Britain

Physical appearance: "Beautiful blue eyes, exquisite nose, pretty mouth, delicate mustache, slight whiskers, elegant figure, broad shoulders, fine waist"

Education: Degree from the University of Bonn, Germany

Languages: German and English

Occupation: Prince consort since February 1840

Income: 50,000 pounds sterling a year requested by the queen but reduced to 30,000 pounds by Parliament

Interests: Music (good organist and composer, according to the composer Felix Mendelssohn), painting (organized the financing for the royal collection of paintings; purchases include Lucas Cranach, Fra Angelico, and Benozzo Gozzoli), architecture, nature (long hikes, hunting, shooting), agriculture (applied modern techniques on the farms of Windsor Castle), botany, apiculture, ice skating, family (goes to bed early), anything related to ethics.

Offices held: Chancellor of Cambridge University

Chairman of the Society of Arts

Chairman of the Society for Improving the Condition of the Laboring Classes

Political activities: Officially limited because of British distrust of his German origins. Tried to help reorganize the army at the outbreak of the Crimean War. Helped prevent war with the United States during the Trent Affair, when a Union ship removed Confederate officials from a British ship; his diplomacy got the Confederates released and averted war.

Proved an excellent adviser to his royal spouse, who made discreet use of his services.

Major achievement: Organized and managed the Great Exhibition of 1851 in which more than a thousand manufactured products, fruits of the Industrial Revolution, were displayed.

Minor achievement: Brought the custom of the Christmas tree to England.

Victoria (Vicky), 17, Edward (Bertie), 16, Alice, 14, Alfred
are happy to announce the birth of their

ENGLISHPEOPLE

(Affie), 13, Helena, 11, Louise, 9, Arthur, 7, and Leopold, 4,
sister Beatrice (Baby), born April 14, 1857.

Victoria's biographers agree on one point: she was extremely conscientious about her job as queen, and though she followed a highly intense work schedule, she did not let business get in the way of her "quality" time as a doting wife and mother.

As for her intellectual interests, the French biographer Abel Chevalley had this to say in 1902: "To be honest, the queen could care less about the matters of the mind. Neither science nor literature interested her. She succeeded, however, in learning a little Hindi in the later part of her life. But her principal form of recreation was playing solitaire, which she found relaxing only if she won. Her primary education removed her from any interests she might have found engaging. After all, she was brought up in an environment that did not encourage intellectual activity. An educated woman was mistrusted, while the fundamental duty of a young girl was to be—or at least appear to be—ignorant. Queen Victoria read only novels and travel books. She was a bad writer. Shades of meaning escaped her. The only thing she asked of a book was that it entertain her—a bit of the picturesque with a touch of feeling thrown in, that was

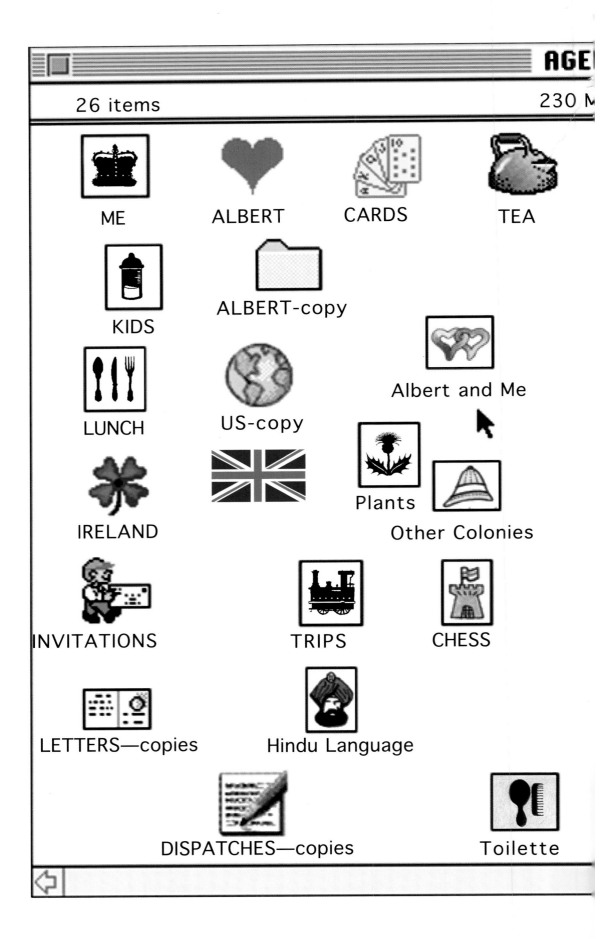

26 items   230 M

ME   ALBERT   CARDS   TEA

KIDS   ALBERT-copy

LUNCH   US-copy   Albert and Me

IRELAND   Plants   Other Colonies

INVITATIONS   TRIPS   CHESS

LETTERS—copies   Hindu Language

DISPATCHES—copies   Toilette

NDA

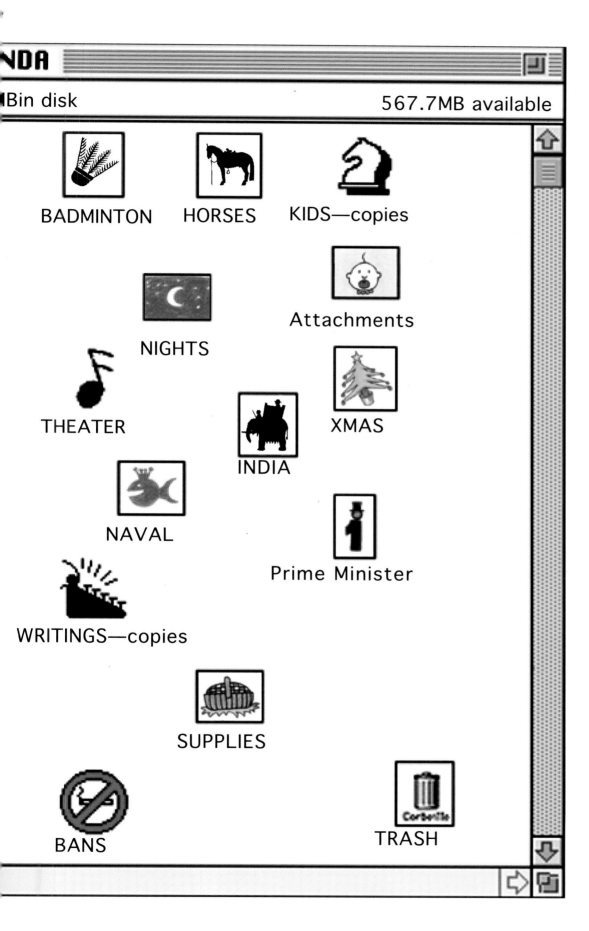

Bin disk   567.7MB available

BADMINTON   HORSES   KIDS—copies

Attachments

NIGHTS

THEATER   XMAS

INDIA

NAVAL

Prime Minister

WRITINGS—copies

SUPPLIES

BANS   TRASH

enough for her. Walter Scott was her favorite author. She liked Jane Austen, too. There were two sides of her nature: on the one hand, an easygoing romanticism, visual, overflowing, without profundity; on the other hand, a bourgeois reality, exacting, somewhat down-to-earth, loyal, and exempt from any philosophical ambition. The queen was more interested in the theater and music. She had a thin voice that she used to maximum capacity. She had known Mendelssohn in all this glory. Mendelssohn had improvised and sung for her and her alone. Prince Albert admired Mendelssohn. For the queen Mendelssohn was the greatest musician in the world. Until her dying day she expressed her absolute contempt for Brahms and Wagner, who nonetheless had their share of champions at the court. When she was told that their music was the wave of the future, she said, 'The future bores me. I don't want to hear any more about it.' Italian music and good light opera delighted her. During her youth, she preferred *Norma*, later it was *Carmen*. At the theater she was all eyes and ears; she followed every twist, every intrigue with the simple, attentive, passionate interest of a child."

THE OTHER HALF

There are really two Englands in Victoria's time. One is the England of aristocrats, wealthy industrialists, and the middle class; the other is the world of the poor and their bitter misery, a life poignantly captured by Charles Dickens (1812-70). His novels are an indictment of a society that grossly mistreated and abused the poor, especially children. In *Oliver Twist*, he writes about the sinister workhouses; in the *Old Curiosity Shop*, about child slavery; in *Nicholas Nickleby*, about the inhuman discipline imposed by the schools of his day. It is in *Hard Times* that Dickens decries the effects of mid-nineteenth-century industrialism in England:

"It was a town of machinery and tall chimneys, out of which interminable serpents of smoke trailed themselves for ever and ever, and never got uncoiled. It had a black canal in it, and a river that ran purple with ill-smelling dye, and vast piles of buildings full of windows where there was a rattling and a trembling all day long, and where the piston of the steam-engine worked monotonously up and down like the head of an elephant in a state of melancholy madness. . . . It contained several large streets all very like one another, and many small streets still more like one another inhabited by people equally like one another, who all went in and out at the same hours, with the same sound upon that same pavement, to do the same work, and to whom every day was the same as yesterday and to-morrow, and every year the counterpart of the last and the next."

The condition of working people is terrible: until 1842 women and children work in mines, and the work day is limited to nine hours only in 1847. Even so, England remains untouched by the revolutionary movements of its European neighbors. Karl Marx publishes his incendiary *Communist Manifesto*, in which he predicts the overthrow of the ruling class by the oppressed workers, in London in 1848, but it creates hardly a ripple in the status quo of Victorian society.

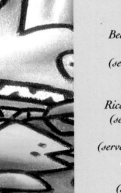

MENU

White soup à la reine
(served with dry sherry)
Bonne bouche of shrimp
Foie gras mousse
Highland salmon
Lobster à la Patti
(served with Sauternes)
Quail en caisse
Balmoral pheasant
Beef tenderloin Prince Albert
Watercress
(served with Pommery 1889)
Targe of lamb
Marinated peas
Rice à la Florence Nightingale
(served with Bollinger 1884)
Ice pudding
(served with Benedictine/Creme de cacao)
Assorted cakes
(served with brandy 1875;
Clos de Vougeot 1888)
Fruit
(served with Château Lafite 1877)
Tea and coffee
(Gallinari/Crofts port 1863)

PROBLEM

Given that this menu for six people was typical fare for the queen, how much of it would she have to eliminate if she wanted to maintain the figure of a young woman whose normal daily intake was 4,000 calories?

WHITE SOUP À LA REINE

Place 1 medium chicken in a cooking pot
Add 3 quarts of chicken stock
Bring to a boil, skim, and salt broth
Add 1 onion studded with a clove, 1 bouquet garni, 1 celery stalk, and $3\frac{1}{2}$ ounces rice
Simmer until the skin of the chicken has separated from the bone
Remove chicken from broth; dice the meat
Remove bouquet garni and onion
Return chicken meat to pot and add $\frac{1}{3}$ pint finely diced vegetables
Bring to boil
Serve hot

FOOD FIT FOR A QUEEN

Victoria's name has often been associated with richly prepared dishes and sauces. Pastry boats and puffs, fillet of sole, poached and soft-boiled eggs, and stuffed omelets Victoria all have these common ingredients: finely diced lobster and truffles. Fish scallops Victoria, for instance, contains mushrooms with truffles covered in a Nantua sauce and decorated with shavings of truffles.

Mixed salad Victoria brings together diced cucumbers and lobster, slivers of celeriac, artichoke hearts, and thin slices of potatoes, with a julienne of truffles and rose mayonnaise seasoning. Garnish Victoria—used for small sautéed meat dishes in a Madeira or port deglazing thickened with veal stock—consists of little tomatoes stuffed with mushroom purée and cooked au gratin, in addition to quartered hearts of artichoke braised in butter. Sauces à la Victoria were used on poached fish (white wine sauce with lobster paste and finely diced lobster and truffle) and venison (a basic brown sauce seasoned with port, red currant jelly, spices, and orange juice).

Solution

Soup (445 calories), bonne bouche of shrimp (600 calories), foie gras mousse (1,100 calories), salmon (1,200 calories), lobster (480 calories), quail (996 calories), pheasant (1,600 calories), beef tenderloin (1,375 calories), watercress (120 calories), lamb (1,428 calories), peas (930 calories), rice (560 calories), ice pudding (2,728 calories), 6 assorted cakes (2,979 calories), 6 pears (660 calories), tea (0 calories), 6 lumps of sugar (120 calories).
Total calories: 17,321.

We know that this meal, which totals 17,321 calories, was prepared for six people; the queen's share was thus one-sixth of the total, or 2,872 calories. We also know that this calculation was based on dishes without sauces. A rich sauce corresponded to about 150 calories per person, and all five main dishes in this meal contained sauces; therefore, we must add 750 calories. It is assumed that the queen did not have bread with her meal but drank on the average three glasses of wine, or 255 calories (85 calories a glass). The queen's total caloric intake for this meal equals 3,877. Considering that she had two meals a day, her grand total would be 7,754 calories. (The queen's continental-style breakfast and high tea did not add much to this total since she hardly touched anything during those meals.)

Important laws enacted include: 1842, tax on income; 1844, Factory Act restricting the working day of women to 12 hours and for children to 6½ hours; 1847, Factory Act reducing the working day to ten hours for women and children between thirteen and eighteen; 1870, Education Act enabling local governments to set up elected school boards that could establish schools supported by local and national taxes; 1871, Trade Union Act guaranteeing legal protection to trade unions; 1880, Education Act making education compulsory up to age ten.

Major strides are made in science and technology during Victoria's reign. Railways crisscross the island; the queen makes the journey to Balmoral Castle in Scotland by train. Thanks to the Great Eastern Company, England and the United States are connected by transatlantic telegraph cable. Michael Faraday studies a new phenomenon, electricity; the astronomer Sir John Herschel catalogs stars;

woman, who swam th[e] [sam]e distance in less than 8 hours.

On June 18, 1840, t[h]e queen faces the first of seven att[e]mpts on her life. A seventeen-y[e]ar-old boy fires a gun at her in h[e]r carriage. Before he has ti[m]e to fire a secon[d] shot, Prince Alb[e]rt pushes the queen down so t[h]at the bull[e]t flies over her head. The queen orders the drivers to c[o]ntinue on to her mother's to rea[s]sure her that she has come to no [h]arm. Days later the queen atten[d]s an opera and is greeted with wil[d] enthusiasm, hats and handke[r]chiefs are waved, and cheering delays the performance f[o]r several minutes.

Lord Shaftesbury (1801-85) spends his life trying to improve the living conditions of the poor. He brings before the government— and a startled public—the pitiful condition of women and children in mines, the terrible conditions of workers' housing, and the urgent need for urban sanitation. Shocked by his experience of the London slums, he takes on the presidency of the Ragged School Union, a confederation of schools that provides basic education, vocational training, and religious instruction to some 300,000 poor, "ragged" children. The statue at Piccadilly Circus is supposedly dedicated to him. Erected in 1886, it is said to represent the angel of charity, but for some unknown reason becomes identified with Cupid, god of erotic love.

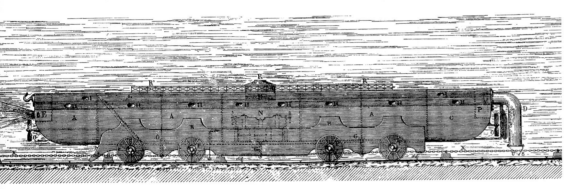

Charles Darwin publishes his Origin of Species in 1859.

The English are said to have an insular mentality, and when the idea of building a tunnel under the English Channel to connect the island with continental Europe is proposed, there is public outcry. Among the staunchest opponents are the poet Tennyson, the archbishop of York, the biologist Thomas Huxley, and the philosopher Herbert Spencer.

The rise in the level of national affluence during the Victorian era does not necessarily translate into better social conditions for all. For instance, the number of servants in Great Britain between 1801 and 1881 jumps from 600,000 to 2 million, indicating that the middle class knows how to enjoy its wealth by contributing to inequality.

The liberal doctrines of laissez-faire and free trade dominate Victorian economy. Industrialization takes off on its own without government interference. In 1846 Robert Peel lifts protectionist laws (Corn Laws) on the export and import of grains into Great Britain and other countries as a result of the efforts of Richard Cobden and his Anti-Corn Law League.

In 1875 Matthew Webb is the first man to swim the English Channel; his time: 21 hours, 45 minutes. The current record holder is a

Around 1892 syphilis, known as the "Russian roulette of Victorian society," is considered the just punishment for the sin of the flesh. It ravages not only the ports where there is a constant flow of sailors, but also London, where the number of prostitutes is estimated at 100,000.

FACT FILE

Prince Albert introduces the tradition of the Christmas tree to England. Christmas cards appear about the same time, in 1840, but do not become popular until the 1870s when they are made more affordable. Charles Dickens writes A Christmas Carol in 1843, and singing carols, some of them composed and arranged by Mendelssohn, is very popular.

Hemophilia, a disease in which the sufferer's blood has trouble clotting, does not spare the royal family. Since the disease is almost always inherited through the female line by male descendants, Queen Victoria is the unwitting carrier of the defective gene. Her son Leopold suffers from the disease, and by the end of the century her children, grandchildren, and great grandchildren have innocently contaminated almost all of the royal families of Europe, including those of Russia and Spain.

Victoria never takes off her mourning clothes after the death of her husband. Nor does she stop erecting monuments in his memory. Among the most spectacular are the famous Albert Memorial in London's Kensington Gardens and the cenotaph at Windsor in which Albert is represented in medieval armor and coat of mail. At Windsor the queen keeps his room just as it was when he was alive; twice a day his clothes are laid out on a chair, soap and towels are replaced, and a hot-water jug is placed steaming on the washstand!

When Lord Melbourne's Whig government falls in 1839, the head of the opposition Tory Party, Sir Robert Peel, sets about forming a new cabinet. The queen dislikes Peel. When the new prime minister insists that the queen dismiss the Whig ladies of the bedchamber who hold important royal household appointments, she refuses. Peel, in turn, gives up his efforts to form a government. The queen then asks Lord Melbourne to return to power. This two-day impasse becomes known as the Bedchamber Crisis.

Napoleon III and Empress Eugenie take great pains to make Queen Victoria at home in the French capital during her triumphant state visit in August 1855. The suite of rooms assigned to Victoria and Albert is redecorated at great expense in white and gold. The queen's room has been designed to resemble, as much as possible, her own at Buckingham Palace. She's thrilled. She is so comfortable, she assures her host the emperor, that apart from the absence of her dog she feels completely at home. No sooner said than done. The emperor sends a courier to London, and three days later the little dog is in the arms of its royal mistress.

The first "underground" railway appears in London in 1863, but not all the kinks have been ironed out: the evacuation of steam presents a real problem. It isn't until 1890, when engineers develop electric engines, that London's subway system grows to be the largest in the world.

Here's what Victoria writes to her uncle Leopold I shortly after the death of her husband: "My own dearest, kindest Father—for as such, have I ever loved you! The poor fatherless baby of eight months is now the utterly broken-hearted and crushed widow of forty-two! My life as a happy one is ended! The world is gone for me! If I must live on (and I will do nothing to make me worse than I am), it is henceforth for our poor fatherless children—for my unhappy country, which has lost all in losing him—and in only doing what I know and feel he would wish, for he is near me—his spirit will guide and inspire me! But oh! to be cut off in the prime of life—to see our pure, happy, quiet domestic life, which alone enabled me to bear my much disliked position, cut off at forty-two—when I had hoped with such instinctive certainty that God never would part us, and would let us grow old together (though he always talked of the shortness of life)—is too awful, too cruel!"

In 1868 London is the largest city in the world but also the dirtiest and most foul-smelling. The streets are still avenues for horses, pigs, and all manner of fowl. Cesspools have been banned since 1848, but open sewers are still everywhere.

When Victoria comes to the throne in 1837 Great Britain has a population of 16 million; at her death sixty-one years later, there are 37 million. This demographic boost is all the more remarkable considering 10 million people leave the country during this period to seek their fortunes elsewhere.

When King Leopold I of Belgium dies in 1865, Victoria loses a second father. Distraught over her loss, she takes a fancy to a Scottish retainer at Balmoral by the name of John Brown. He becomes her bodyguard of sorts, following her everywhere, helping her into her carriage or onto her horse, and putting on her coat. Occasionally the queen asks him for his opinion, sometimes on very important matters. Neither educated nor especially intelligent, Brown has a reputation as a heavy drinker. It is probable that Victoria, who has become a devotee of the then fashionable spiritualism after the death of her husband, feels closer to her beloved Albert's spirit when Brown, who served the prince, is nearby. Plausible as this may be, John Brown's continued presence in the queen's company gives rise to endless gossip.

CLOVER DOESN'T ALWAYS HAVE FOUR LEAVES (IRELAND)

The Act of Union of 1800 formally unites Great Britain and Ireland. The Irish Parliament is abolished, and Ireland is represented in the British Parliament. But this union does not put an immediate end to British colonial involvement in Irish life. Nor does it help improve that country's already dire social and economic conditions. In fact, the lack of coal makes Ireland very dependent on England.

The stability of Ireland on the social, national, and religious fronts is extremely precarious when Victoria takes the throne. The Catholic Emancipation Act of 1829, which gives Irish Catholics the right to sit in Parliament, does little to ease the tension between the two countries. Daniel O'Connell, member of Parliament and perhaps the greatest political personality in nineteenth-century Ireland, organizes a nonviolent campaign against the Act of Union that reaches its peak in 1843 at a huge meeting on the old royal hill of Tara when more than half a million of O'Connell's supporters gather. The sight of hundreds of thousands of Irishmen dressed in "Repealer coats" and marching in military formation terrifies the English. The British government bans a huge planned meeting scheduled later that same year at Clontarf, and O'Connell bows to the order. But everything that happens in Ireland in the nineteenth century is overshadowed by the catastrophe that overtakes the country between 1845 and 1849, a disaster that poisons relations between Ireland and England for generations to come and has the most profound effects in Ireland itself. This is the potato famine, also known as the great hunger. The root of this misery lay in the dependence of the country on just one staple crop, the potato, and the villain is a fungus brought to Ireland by ship from America. The blight spreads with such sinister speed that within three years Ireland's entire potato crop is nearly wiped out. The British government responds to this calamity with such inadequate measures that its policy is severely condemned and labeled by Irish historians as nothing less than genocide by willful neglect. By 1852 more than 1.6 million people have died of starvation and disease, and nearly another 2 million Irish have emigrated, most of them to the United States.

Irish property passes into the hands of a new class of landlords who are unsympathetic to the interests of the local population. In 1881 half of the 600,000 farms in Ireland are no larger than 25 acres while disproportionately half the country is in the hands of just 750 major landowners. The catastrophe of the potato famine and the misery that follows result in 1858 in the formation of the clandestine revolutionary group called the Irish Republican Brotherhood—also known as the Fenians—which pledges itself to home rule and the violent overthrow of English rule in Ireland. The Home Rule movement seeks to regain Irish control of internal affairs by reestablishing the Irish Parliament. A supporter of Irish autonomy, Gladstone introduces a Home Rule bill in 1886, but controversy over the measure eventually brings down his government and he is replaced by Salisbury as prime minister.

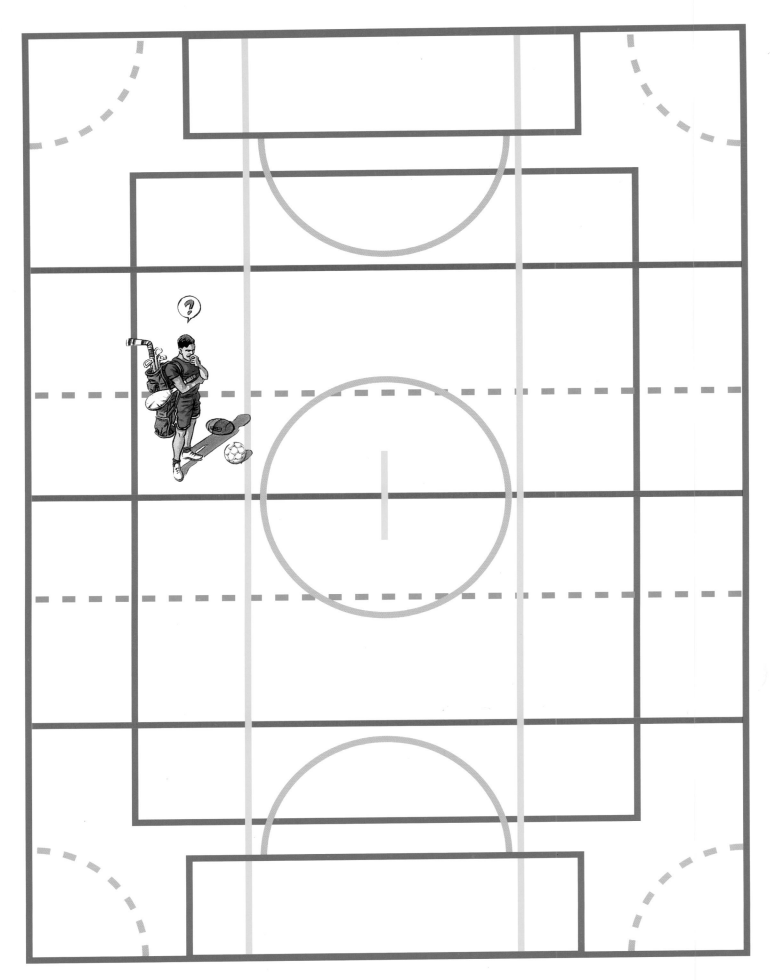

SPORTS

By the end of the nineteenth century, the English are beginning to pay more attention to their bodies; they realize that outdoor activities are good for the mind, too. One detail, though: this observation is made by the privileged class; everyone else is too busy toiling.

Team sports are all the rage because they bring into play the spirit of discipline and competition, as well as endurance, considered to be the number-one character-building qualities of the time. Among the new athletic disciplines of the age, the following are worth noting: squash, which is invented in 1850 by students of Harrow; basketball, which originates in the United States; and lawn tennis, which is developed in England in 1874 by Major Walter Wingfield. The first championship tournament of tennis is organized in 1877 at Wimbledon on a croquet field.

Rugby is played for the first time around 1840 on the fields of a prep school called (big surprise) Rugby. Though the game of cricket originated in medieval times, it is regarded in Victorian England as a unifying national symbol. W. G. Grace is one of its star players. He is said to have scored 54,896 runs during his long career. The English import polo from India in 1862 (the word comes from the Tibetan *pulu*, which means "willow root"). From 1839 onward the leisurely class enjoy the Henley regatta on the Thames River, while the Cambridge-Oxford race becomes a popular annual event as of 1856.

The less privileged classes fall back on soccer. In fact, it makes its first appearance on the streets of working-class districts in large cities. Very quickly, though, the sport is codified, and the first soccer association comes into being in 1863.

Not to be forgotten is bicycling, which is taken up more and more by women. How do they manage to do it in corset and crinoline? The crowning point of the age is the revival of the Olympic Games in Athens in 1896 after an interruption of 1,500 years. Only twelve competitive events are staged, all of them restricted to men. Women are not allowed to compete in the games until 1912.

HANDS OFF MY ISLAND

"Not only England, but every Englishman is an island," wrote the eighteenth-century German poet Novalis. Is it this sense of insularity that makes the English feel so safe and superior? And is it their fierce spirit of independence that contributes to their belief that they are the center of the world and no one and nothing can touch them?

The year 1830: there is revolution in France and Belgium; 1848: revolution in France, Italy, and Germany; 1849: revolution in Hungary and Italy. And in England? Nothing happens. Yet the economic and social crises are there, and the same murmurings of revolt are in the air. This situation leads philosopher Friedrich Engels to state in 1844 that revolution is around the corner. But nothing happens. Historians have presented a dozen or so hypotheses to explain why nothing happened, and the psychological explanation prevails: due to their insularity, the English are fanatically independent and inclined to keep away from any influences beyond the English Channel. They also have a deep-seated respect for the established order and an implicit trust in a ruling elite. French historian François Bedarida made note of this complacency in writing about the Great Exhibition of 1851: "Isn't it touching just to contemplate all those fustian jackets and badly shaved English chins there on the lawns of Hyde Park quietly picnicking instead of thinking about revolutionizing society when all the implements of a triumphant capitalism are only a stone's throw away?"

This English detachment applies to foreign affairs, too. Except for the Crimean War, the country remains uninvolved in the conflicts that shake the continent between 1814 and 1914. British diplomacy is certainly at work during this period, its goal to keep Britain out of any entanglements with its continental neighbors and to stay out of alliances with other great powers. Victoria and her various ministers are primarily interested with pursuing an imperial gameplan of building the empire. The British army at this time is tiny compared with those of the other European powers, the English relying on their naval power to maintain their position of strength and containment. Victorian diplomacy from 1885 to 1900 is defined by the policy of "splendid isolation," a phrase associated with the name of Lord Salisbury, who is prime minister during most of this time. The message is clear: England wants a stable Europe but does not want any complicated alliances.

If there's one word that best describes Victorian interior decoration it's *eclectic*—and that's putting it mildly! The Victorians don't like empty spaces, and with knickknacks available from every corner of the British Empire, there is something for every shelf. The Industrial Revolution does its share, too, providing plenty of imitations. The Victorians want to have reproductions of all the best the past has to offer, and they also revive artisan traditions.

ORIGINAL ANTIQUES

The Victorians' answer to the elegant neoclassical style of the Regency period that preceded it is clutter. Furniture is massive and ornate, with motifs drawn from different historical periods rioting all over: chairs and tables are decorated with inlaid marble, mother-of-pearl, or a profusion of carving, and overstuffed sofas and armchairs are upholstered in velvet and brocade. This "high style" lasts until 1900.

STAMP OF APPROVAL

Before the postage stamp, there was the postmark. In England it takes the form of a triangular impression in red ink bearing the words "Penny post paid." From 1834 to 1838 an Englishman by the name of Chalmers, a printer and bookseller in Dundee, prints a kind of postage label of which he was the inventor. But the real father of the postage stamp is Rowland Hill. In 1837 he publishes a pamphlet entitled *Post Office Reform* in which he proposes that letters be carried any distance within Great Britain and Ireland for a fixed rate, and that all postage be prepaid (at the time most letters go through post unpaid, to be collected on delivery). Wrappers and envelopes with the stamp denoting prepayment are to be sold at all post offices, and for people who want to use their own stationery, Hill proposes "a bit of paper just large enough to bear the stamp [imprint of the post office hand stamp] and covered at the back with a glutinous wash, which might, by applying a little moisture, attach to the back of the letter."

Hill's proposal is submitted to the Houses of Parliament, where it meets great resistance. Thanks to the publicity generated by the press, Hill is able to work out the details of his proposal to everyone's satisfaction. On August 17, 1839, a law is passed authorizing the use of the adhesive postage stamp, and a competition is held. The subject chosen for the stamp is, of course, Queen Victoria. Henry Courbould makes a drawing from a portrait that was used by the royal mint for the medal struck commemorating the queen's first visit to London in 1837. Above the head of the queen is the word "Postage" and below is a panel with "One Penny" or "Two Penny." Engraved by Charles and Frederick Heaths, the stamp is printed in London by Perkins, Bacon, and Petch. On May 6, 1840, both stamps are ready: the one-penny is black, the two-penny blue.

The following year these stamps are sold in every post office in Great Britain. In the colonies they bear a postmark with a letter and number to indicate where the stamps have been issued; this system continues until 1881. The postage stamp is enthusiastically adopted by the British public: in 1839, 50 million letters are sent within the country; in 1840, 170 million, and ten years later, more than double that number!

The celebrated one-penny black and its companion, the two-penny blue, are now among the rarest stamps in the world and the prize of any collection.

I ♥ PARIS

In September 1843 Victoria and Albert set sail in the royal yacht to visit King Louis Philippe at the Chateau d'Eu in Normandy. It is the first time the queen has set foot in Europe and the first official visit of a British sovereign to France since Henry VIII met Francis I on the Field of the Cloth of Gold in 1520.

In April 1855 the recently proclaimed emperor of the French, Napoleon III, pays a visit to Windsor with his wife, the Empress Eugenie. The royal couples get along so well that Victoria and Albert pay a return visit to Paris four months later. They arrive at the Gare de Strasbourg on the evening of August 18. "I felt quite bewildered but enchanted," she notes in her journal. "It was like a fairy tale, and everything so beautiful!" In honor of her arrival, Paris has been transformed: the queen passes through a forest of flags and banners, and every thousand yards or so, vast archways of imitation marble, garlands, and coats of arms span the wide boulevards. Everywhere enormous Napoleonic eagles glitter in gold. The open carriage drives through cheering crowds around the Place de la Concorde, up the Champs-Elysees, under the Arc de Triomphe, through the Bois de Boulogne, and on to the palace of Saint Cloud. All along the route cannons roar, bands play "God Save the Queen," trumpets sound, and crowds shout, *"Vive la Reine d'Angleterre!" "Vive l'Empereur!" "Vive le Prince Albert!"*

The emperor spares no effort to make the visit magical. The suite of rooms assigned to Victoria and Albert—once the apartments of Queen Marie Antoinette—have been especially redecorated in white and gold to remind them of Buckingham Palace. Napoleon has even given orders that the legs of the table that belonged to the French queen be cut short to fit his diminutive guest. Sumptuous Gobelins tapestries cover the walls, and from the garden below the sound of fountains and the scent of orange blossoms fill the air. "I have such a home feeling," the queen assures her host. Everything is charming.

The coffee is excellent. The furniture is "so well stuffed," Victoria notes, "that by lying a little while on the sofa, you are completely rested." The cornices, gilded in no fewer than three different shades of gold, are truly magnificent. In a letter to her uncle Leopold, the queen writes: "I am delighted, enchanted, amused, and interested, and think I never saw anything more beautiful and gay than Paris—or more splendid than all the palaces. Our reception is most gratifying—for it is enthusiastic and really kind in the highest degree. . . . How beautiful and enjoyable this place is!"

The most dramatic moment of the queen's visit takes place at the Hotel des Invalides, where she goes to see the tomb of the great Napoleon. "There I stood," she writes afterward, "at the arm of Napoleon III, his nephew, before the coffin of England's bitterest foe; I, the granddaughter of that king who hated him most, and who most vigorously opposed him, and this very nephew, who bears his name, being my nearest and dearest ally!"

The queen is so moved by the occasion, in which "old enmities and rivalries" are wiped out, that she instructs the prince of Wales to kneel beside the coffin.

The "delightful and never-to-be-forgotten" visit to Paris ends with a great ball at Versailles. "Of the splendor of the fete at Versailles, I can really give no impression, for it exceeded all imagination!" enthuses the queen.

"It's terrible that there's only one more night," sighs the emperor. Victoria agrees and begs him to come soon again to England.

"Most certainly!" he answers. "Now that we know each other, we can visit each other at Windsor or Fontainebleau without any ceremony, can't we?" This would give her great pleasure, Victoria says. She laughingly assures him that she will return the following year as an ordinary traveler, take a cab, and present herself at the Tuileries to beg some dinner.

AUSTRALIA AND NEW ZEALAND

The first settlement in Australia is a penal colony for "transported" British convicts. It is established in 1788 in an area in southeastern Australia called New South Wales at what is now Sydney. Convicts continue to be sent to Australia, and in 1830, 50,000 more of them land on its shores. Essentially, the British government is colonizing the country in order to rid itself of its "bad guys." More colonies are settled as more of the island continent is charted. By the middle of the nineteenth century free colonization has replaced the old penal settlements. New South Wales is only the first in a series of colonies that later unite to form modern Australia: Tasmania (1825), Western Australia (1829), South Australia (1834), Victoria (1851), and Queensland (1859). Australia's greatest economic boom occurs when sheep raising for wool production becomes an industry. As the white settlers advance inland to occupy new grazing land, the indigenous Aborigines are forced farther inland, their tribes disintegrating when their traditional organization collapses and their hunting grounds are invaded. In 1851 a major gold strike brings a flood of settlers into southeastern Australia, contributing to the rapid growth of Melbourne. The push for vast tracts of grazing land for sheep and cattle spurs the development of railroads, and by the 1890s more than 10,000 miles of track have been laid. New discoveries of copper, silver, and gold drive economic development at a fast pace. Australia is a cornucopia of riches. Urbanization, industrialization, and the fear of foreign incursions, leading to restrictions on Asian immigration, fuel the movement toward unification of the colonies. Federal union is delayed because of rivalries among the six colonies. Finally, an Australian constitution is accepted, and the Commonwealth of Australia, with domestic self-government and continuing allegiance to the British crown, comes into being in 1901.

Australia's neighbor New Zealand achieves dominion status in 1907. The country has been occupied by the Maori since before 1400. When the first permanent European settlement is established at Wellington in 1840, the Maori sign a treaty recognizing British sovereignty in exchange for guaranteed possession of their land. The colonial settlers, however, soon clash with the Maoris, a situation that causes Queen Victoria great concern. She sends Sir George Grey to act as governor. He believes that economic development can be achieved only if the country has a strong central government. Loans are secured to pay for the construction of roads and bridges, and this indebtedness causes a serious economic crisis until 1895, when refrigeration allows the country to finally export dairy products to Great Britain.

THE GREAT EXHIBITION

May 1, 1851, is one of the most glorious days of Victoria's reign. It is also the crowning achievement of her dearly beloved husband Albert's career, for he is the father of the first international trade show.

Of the 220 proposals submitted for a pavilion, it is English gardener Joseph Paxton's design in glass, christened the Crystal Palace, that is chosen. An immense 108-foot-high greenhouse, modeled on a conservatory Paxton designed in the late 1830s and using newly developed techniques for making large panes of glass, the building is 1,848 feet long—more than a third of a mile—and 408 feet wide. Objections to Hyde Park as the site of the "palace of glass" are quelled when Paxton adjusts the plans so that trees will be enclosed rather than cut down, thus protecting the aesthetics of the park. The queen is full of admiration for the exhibition, in particular for her husband's organizational skills. She writes to her uncle King Leopold of Belgium: "I wish you could have witnessed the first of May, the greatest day in our history, the most beautiful and inspiring and touching spectacle ever seen, and the triumph of my beloved Albert. Truly it was astonishing, a fairy scene. Many cried, and all felt touched and impressed with devotional feelings. It was the happiest, proudest day in my life, and I can think of nothing else. Albert's dearest name is immortalized with this great conception, his own, and my own dear country showed she was worthy of it." The exhibition is a great success, and Prince Albert has every reason to be proud, despite many complaints that some objects on display—such as the replica of Osborne House carved in coal, the statue of the queen in zinc, and several stuffed frogs—are in bad taste. In fact, not everyone shares the queen's enthusiasm for the exhibition. Lord Palmerston opposes the project from the start and maintains his position up to the end, even in the face of its enormous financial success. Noticing that sparrows are roosting in the trees in the Crystal Palace and spoiling the display stands, the queen sends for the duke of Wellington and asks him what to do. Not one to beat around the bush, the victor of Waterloo replies, "Sparrow hawks, Ma'am."

The great nineteenth-century poet Tennyson captures the popular enthusiasm for the exhibition in these words: "Uplift a thousand voices full and swell, In this wide hall with earth's invention stored, And praise the invisible Lord, Who lets once more in peace the nations meet, Where Science, Art, and Labour have outpour'd their myriad horns of plenty at our feet."

In six months, 6 million visitors from all over the world come to London to see this magical place. The queen herself goes back forty times!

This exhibition, with its 109,000 items on display and its 14,000 participants, nearly half of them from abroad, celebrates with pomp and circumstance the triumph of industrial England, the age of the machine, and a royal couple at the height of its reign.

TRAVELS OF A QUEEN

NORTH
SEA

BELGIUM

DARMSTADT

BADEN-
BADEN

LUCERNE

LAKE MAGGIORE

Queen Victoria has a passion for travel. Most of all she likes to travel by train among her favorite residences, including Windsor Castle; Osborne House, her seaside home on the Isle of Wight; and Balmoral Castle in the Scottish Highlands, where she often goes in the summer. She also travels across the English Channel to visit Europe, and when staying abroad for any length of time she insists on taking along her bed and desk, a complete gallery of family portraits, and one of her carriages with several horses. On such trips she is accompanied by over sixty people, including her French chef, doctors, secretaries, and ladies-in-waiting. She often spends the winter in Nice and Cannes, as well as in the resorts of Aix-les-Bains and Biarritz. Though she travels incognito as the countess of Balmoral, few people mistake the majestic elderly lady in black for anyone but the queen of England. In France, she is loved and respected and is known as *Madame d'Angleterre* ("Mrs. England"). During one stay there she visits the monastery of La Grande Chartreuse, which is perched some 3,000 feet up a mountain and thus involves a risky journey over steep roads. The adventurous queen makes the ascent and is interested in everything she sees. She is particularly intrigued by a young Englishman who joined the order soon after turning eighteen. When they meet, he kneels, kisses her hand, and tells her he is proud to be her subject. The queen, who even in old age has an eye for a handsome youth, notes in her diary that he is "very good-looking and tall, with rather a delicate complexion and a beautiful, saintly, almost rapt expression." Of all the places Queen Victoria visits in her lifetime, it is the Scottish Highlands that truly capture her heart, and it is there that her happiest days are spent. Here's what she has to say about one visit: "We mounted at once . . . and rode on for two hours up Glen Geldie. The hills were wild, but not very high, bare of trees. . . . As you approach [Fishie] glen, which is very narrow, the scenery becomes very fine. The rapid river is overhung by rocks, with trees, birch and fir; the hills, as you advance, rise very steeply on both sides, with rocks and corries, and occasional streamlets falling from very high—while the path winds along, rising gradually higher and higher. It is quite magnificent!" (September 4, 1860). "The falls of the Stron-na-Barin, with that narrow steep glen, which you ride up, crossing at the bottom, were in great beauty. We stopped before we entered the wood, and lunched on the bank overhanging the river. . . .We walked a short way, and then remounted our ponies; but as we were to keep on the other side of the river, not by the Invereshie huts, we had to get off for a few hundred yards, the path being so narrow as to make it utterly unsafe to ride. . . .The huts, surrounded by magnificent fir-trees, and by quantities of juniper-bushes, looked lovelier than ever; and we gazed with sorrow at their utter ruin. I felt what a delightful little encampment it must have been, and how enchanting to live in such a spot as this beautiful solitary wood in a glen surrounded by the high hills" (October 8, 1861).

LOVE STORY
(Continuation and end)

December 12, 1861. Albert has been ill for nearly a month with what the doctors diagnose as typhoid fever, at that time a common and very dangerous disease. On this day his temperature has risen, and he is often delirious. He thinks he hears the birds singing at Rosenau, the place of his birth, near Coburg. On Friday the thirteenth "the breathing was the alarming thing," Victoria writes, "it was so rapid. There was what they call a dusky hue about the face and hands, which I knew was not good." Albert is sinking fast. The queen collapses in uncontrollable grief. When she recovers, she sits calmly by his bed. The prince regains consciousness. He kisses his wife, presses her hand, and calls her "*gutes Fräuchen* [good little wife]." On the fourteenth Albert's breathing worsens. Victoria bends over him and says, "*Es is das kleine Fräuchen* [It is your little wife]." She asks him for "*ein Kuss* [a kiss]." He kisses her, then sinks into sleep. Victoria bursts into tears. Shortly before eleven that evening Prince Albert dies. He is forty-two years old. "Oh, yes, this is death!" Victoria cries on seeing her husband. "I know it. I have seen it before." The queen breaks down completely and for months after her family and ministers fear for her sanity.

But the queen's great sense of duty to her country and her firm belief in an afterlife enable her to carry on. Though she will mourn Albert for the rest of her life, her spiritual bond with him and absolute faith in their reunion after her death give her courage.

49

"WE ARE NOT AMUSED"

The Victorian era has often been branded as straitlaced, repressive, and moralistic—and the description is not far from the truth. After all, what can you say about a society that drapes the legs and feet of all tables so as to obscure any reference to the human body? And what can you say about the declaration of a certain Doctor William Acton in 1857 that "The majority of women (happily for society) are not very much troubled with sexual feeling of any kind"?

The highly reliable Chambers dictionary offers a similar opinion about what it means to be Victorian: "strict but somewhat conventional in morals, with connotations of prudery, solemnity, and sometimes hypocrisy." And no one embodied these characteristics more than the queen herself, influenced as she was by the strict Germanic discipline imposed by her beloved Albert. Paradoxically, these traits became even more pronounced after the prince consort's death. Victoria never came out of formal mourning for her husband. She never again appeared dressed in anything but her solemn black dresses and her widow's cap—as decades went on she came to personify the idea of the Victorian widow—and she imposed a similarly austere life on court. The famous early twentieth-century biographer Lytton Strachey had this to say: "The due distinctions of rank were immaculately preserved. The queen's mere presence was enough to ensure that; but, in addition, the dominion of court etiquette was paramount. . . . Every evening after dinner, the hearth-rug, sacred to royalty, loomed before the profane in inaccessible glory, or, on one or two terrific occasions, actually lured them magnetically forward to the very edge of the abyss. The Queen, at the fitting moment, moved towards her guests; one after the other they were led up to her; and, while dialogue followed dialogue in constraint and embarrassment, the rest of the assembly stood still, without a word. Only in one particular was the severity of the etiquette allowed to lapse. Throughout the greater part of the reign the rule that ministers must stand during their audiences with the Queen had been absolute. When Lord Derby, the Prime Minister, had an audience of Her Majesty after a serious illness, he mentioned it afterwards, as a proof of the royal favor, that the Queen had remarked 'How sorry she was she could not ask him to be seated.'"

Most of the anecdotes and legends about Queen Victoria come to us from this time, including her celebrated "We are not amused," her blood-chilling rebuke to any off-color remark. One of the stories of how this phrase came into existence concerns a Lieutenant Bruce, a young Indian subaltern in the British army in India, who was in the personal service of the queen. One evening during dinner, he ventured to tell a story with a spice of scandal or impropriety in it to his neighbor. The burst of laughter that ensued drew the attention of the queen, who demanded to know the reason for the outburst. Mortified, Bruce had to repeat the story, and when he had finished the queen is said to have pronounced her celebrated statement.

ISN'T IT ROMANTIC?

Left: *Rain, Steam, Speed*, by Turner. Above and below: *Pandora* and *La Ghulandala* by Rossetti. Center: *Ophelia* by Millais.

It isn't easy for the English painters of the time to express their true feelings about nature and to break away from the conventions that taught them to paint idealized landscapes. One of the first to free himself from these shackles is John Constable (1776-1837). Fascinated by the ever-changing moods of nature, he is far more interested in such changes than in the things that stay the same in a given view. The freedom of his brushwork, his spontaneous evocation of sunlight and rain, of storms and passing clouds, represent a new way of looking at nature. For William Turner (1775-1851), the other great English landscapist of the time, this feeling is translated in spectacular, fantastic effects. Seeing everything in nature through intensely human eyes, he fills his paintings with light in which forms lose their structure and definition. Turner is said to have once had himself strapped to the mast of a ship during a storm so he could better translate that feeling to canvas. This spirit of artistic adventure is certainly not lost on a group of young painters and sculptors who in 1848 found the Pre-Raphaelite Brotherhood (P.R.B.) in London: John Everett Millais, William Holman Hunt, and Dante Gabriel Rossetti. They choose this name because they want to revive in British painting the purity and simplicity of Italian painting before Raphael's move to Rome. The movement is a blend of romantic medievalism, in which the study of nature and the heartfelt expression of ideas are precepts, and its goal is to turn painting into a moral as well as an aesthetic act. The PRB revives the early Flemish technique of applying layer on layer of translucent color to capture detail in light. The brotherhood's hyperrealistic works provoke widespread anger and criticism at the time, but later gain popularity and are even copied. The queen, whose tastes are conventionally classical, does not like the Pre-Raphaelites and refuses to have her portrait painted by one of them.

Economic prosperity, more than any other single factor, best defines mid-Victorian Britain. Considered the "workshop of the world," Britain is responsible at the time for one-third of the world's manufactured goods. Two-thirds of the world's coal, half of its cotton manufacture, and 40 percent of its hardware also come from Britain, and by 1870 half the world's steel. Blessed with an abundance of natural resources, particularly coal and iron, the country also holds a position of strength on the high seas of international trade and has a highly effective sales network all across Europe. The United Kingdom reigns supreme.   Transportation is everywhere at work. Steamships and railways transform life, providing inexpensive travel and encouraging heavy industry. Railways unite a society once composed of separate regions and counties and promote urbanization. Steamships bring back from abroad the raw materials so vital to the workshop of the world. In 1851 Britain's gross national product is worth 523 million pounds; in 1870, 916 million pounds. This economic miracle means that at midcentury the per capita income of the British has jumped from 25 pounds to 35, at a time when France's is 21 pounds and Germany's 13 pounds.

But beyond the resources and innovations that contribute to this remarkable prosperity, how can this "Victorian supremacy"—this confidence in the present and faith in the idea of progress—be explained? After all, it has had an impact on the history of Great Britain ever since. Even Margaret Thatcher made reference to it in her attempt to invigorate British economy and society.

Without doubt, the spirit of invention and initiative of the new industrialists—those dynamic entrepreneurs who go on to found large companies like Boots pharmacy and Cadbury chocolates—contributes to the nation's unchallenged supremacy. In addition, the government during this time promotes free trade, thus stimulating competition. According to French historian François Bedarida, other contributing factors were "human resources characterized by advanced technological know-how, sound scientific development, a system of learning that favored empiricism and innovation, and absolute confidence in the merits of competition."

The Great Exhibition, the first international fair in history, opens in London on May 1, 1851, and is Britain's showcase for the world's industrial and artistic products and a monument to free trade. Of the 14,000 exhibitors at the fair, half are from the United Kingdom. Among the contributions are dazzling feats of engineering, such as hydraulic presses and steam engines, in addition to furniture, musical instruments, jewelry (visitors are particularly enthralled by the 186-karat Koh-i-Nor diamond), and agricultural machinery.

After 1873, economic and political events begin to undermine the Victorian belief that all is well. The press calls this period of falling prices and profits the "Great Depression." But in retrospect Britain was not the only country to feel the effects of the boom and bust created by the liberal capitalism of the day. Other countries in Europe have their own share of economic problems, though in Britain's case, the crisis does not really translate into a depression as it was characterized then, but only a slower growth rate.

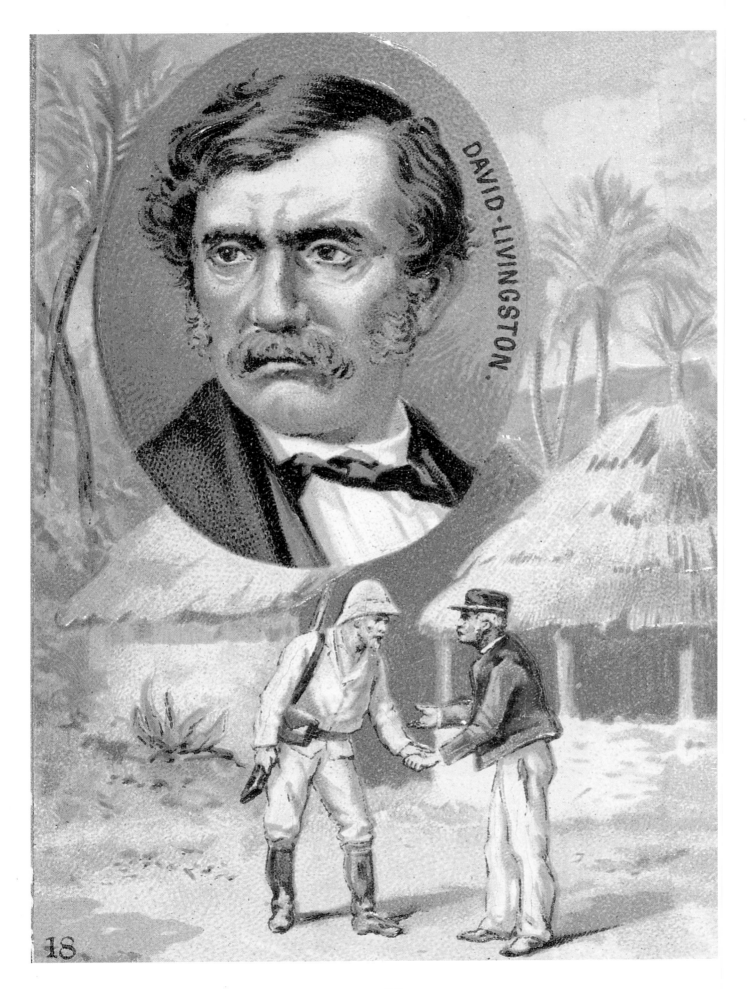

DAVID·LIVINGSTON.

18

DOCTOR LIVINGSTONE, I PRESUME?

Africa is the last continent to succumb to the European explorer, missionary, trader, and soldier. From the 1840s to the 1880s, British explorers lead expeditions that chart the African interior. Missionaries follow, convinced that Africans will benefit from European civilization. Adventurers make fortunes overnight. "Darkest Africa" is rapidly being illuminated by Europe and the schemes of Europeans.

One of the greatest explorers of the time is David Livingstone. Born in Scotland in 1813 to a family of humble background, Livingstone goes to work in a cotton mill at age ten. He teaches himself Latin, goes to college, and gets a medical degree in 1840. That year he is ordained by the London Missionary Society and is sent to its northernmost station, in Bechuanaland in southern Africa. Livingstone's dream is to bring Christianity to the people and relieve human suffering. He opens a school and a clinic. In 1849 he pushes northward, past Lake Ngami, and is the first European to see the Zambezi River. Six years later, while following the course of the Zambezi, he comes across a spectacular sight: a waterfall that is about a mile wide with a drop of 350 feet. The natives call it *mossi-oa-tounia* ("thundering smoke"); Livingstone names it Victoria Falls.

On his return to England to 1856, Livingstone publishes his best-seller, *Missionary Researches and Travels in South Africa*. The following year he is appointed consul for Africa's east coast and goes back

with the express purpose of wiping out the slave trade and exploring the mountainous country of Nyasaland. It is on this expedition that he "discovers" Lake Nyasa.

After a brief stay in England, Livingstone launches yet another African expedition, this time to central Africa in search of the sources of the Zambezi, Congo, and Nile rivers. In 1870 he finds himself near a large river that the natives called Loualaba; no one can tell him whether this river flows east toward the Nile, or west toward the Congo. It is at this time that Livingstone loses touch with the world and is feared dead. "Where is Livingstone? Is he alive or dead?" run the headlines in all the London papers. In 1871 the *New York Herald* commissions the English-born journalist Henry Morton Stanley to find Livingstone. Arriving in Zanzibar on January 26, 1871, Stanley immediately proceeds to investigate Livingstone's whereabouts. Ten months later, on the eastern bank of Lake Tanganyika, Stanley spots a white man coming toward him.

"Doctor Livingstone, I presume?" Stanley asks, not believing his eyes.

"Yes," the man says with a kind smile, lifting his hat slightly.

Although ill, Livingstone refuses to return to England. He is determined to find the source of the Nile. On August 25, 1872, he leaves Lake Tanganyika and makes his way north, convinced that the river's source is to be found in the region of Lake Bangweulu. But his forces give out before he can reach a conclusion. He is found dead in his hut on May 1, 1873. His followers carry his body 1,500 miles to the British consul at Zanzibar, and from there he is brought to lie in Westminster Abbey, a hero.

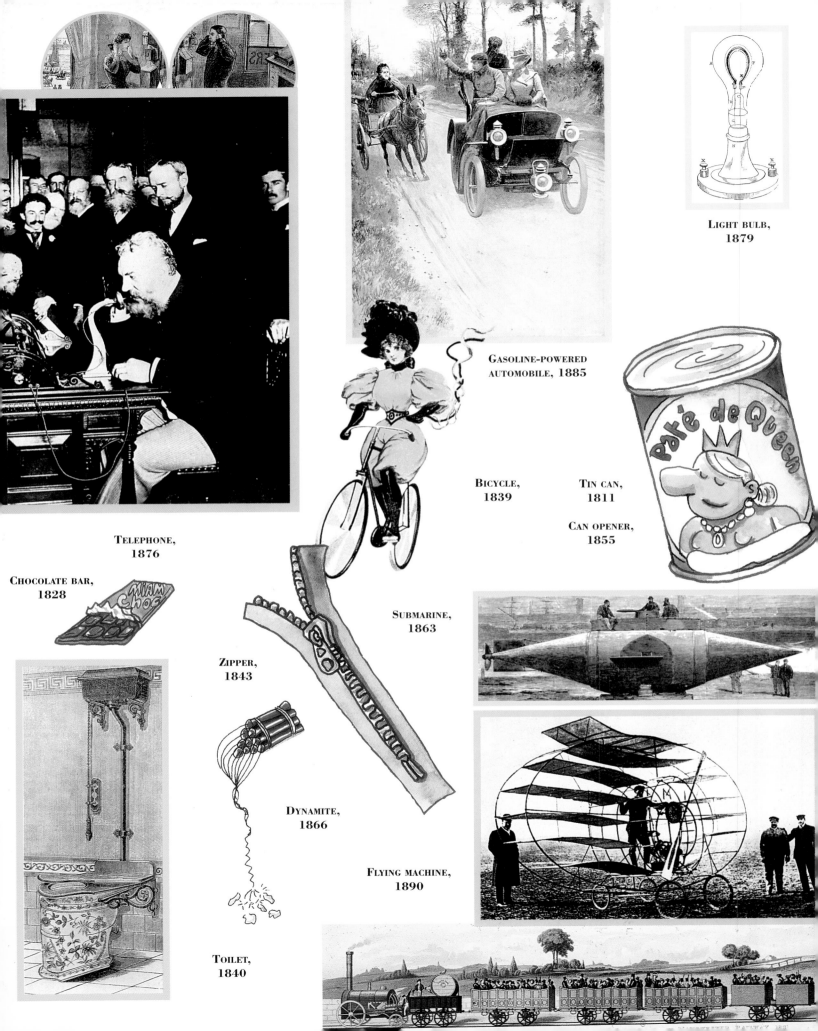

LIGHT BULB,
1879

GASOLINE-POWERED
AUTOMOBILE, 1885

TELEPHONE,
1876

BICYCLE,
1839

TIN CAN,
1811

CAN OPENER,
1855

CHOCOLATE BAR,
1828

ZIPPER,
1843

SUBMARINE,
1863

DYNAMITE,
1866

FLYING MACHINE,
1890

TOILET,
1840

A CENTURY OF INVENTION AND DISCOVERY

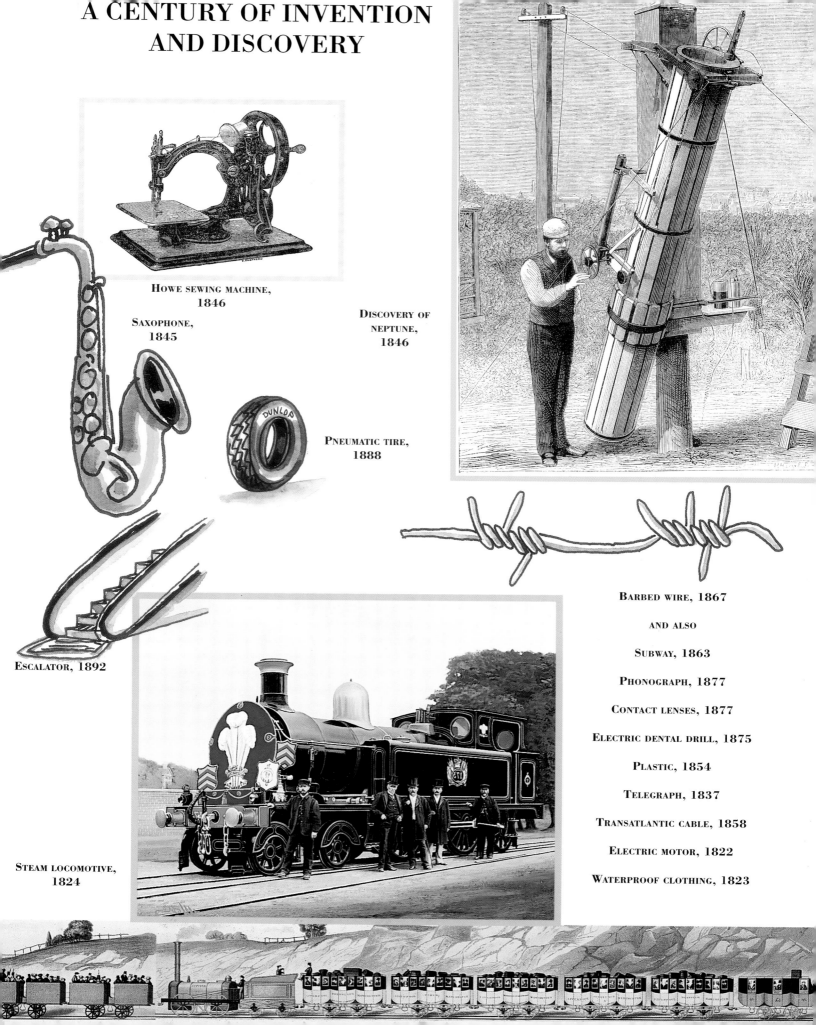

HOWE SEWING MACHINE, 1846

SAXOPHONE, 1845

DISCOVERY OF NEPTUNE, 1846

PNEUMATIC TIRE, 1888

ESCALATOR, 1892

STEAM LOCOMOTIVE, 1824

BARBED WIRE, 1867

AND ALSO

SUBWAY, 1863

PHONOGRAPH, 1877

CONTACT LENSES, 1877

ELECTRIC DENTAL DRILL, 1875

PLASTIC, 1854

TELEGRAPH, 1837

TRANSATLANTIC CABLE, 1858

ELECTRIC MOTOR, 1822

WATERPROOF CLOTHING, 1823

ELEMENTARY,

JACK THE RIPPER

Between August 31 and November 9, 1888, at least five, perhaps seven, prostitutes are brutally murdered in London's East End neighborhood. The murderer gets his nickname, Jack the Ripper, when police receive notes about the killings from someone calling himself by that name. Those suspected of being the Ripper include a pastor, a policeman, the attorney Montague John Druitt (who commits suicide after the last murder), even Queen Victoria's grandson the duke of Clarence, his friend John Stephen, and Sir William Gull, physician to the royal family. Jack the Ripper is one of the first sexual criminals recorded in the history of crime. Even Sherlock Holmes may not have been able to catch him since cases of sexual deviance were not his forte: he preferred inheritance cases. Terror grips London during Jack's gruesome career. The police force in England is less than ideal at the time, with one policeman for every 769 inhabitants. Scotland Yard saturates the area with police, and vigilantes roam the streets. Despite all these efforts the Ripper is never arrested, and his identity remains a mystery to this day.

MY DEAR WATSON!

Sir Arthur Conan Doyle, creator of Sherlock Holmes, is born in Edinburgh, Scotland, in 1859. Doyle begins his career as a doctor specializing in ophthalmology, but when his medical practice falters, he starts writing to augment his income. Sherlock Holmes sees the light of day in 1887 with the publication of the novel *A Study in Scarlet*. The first of the celebrated detective's adventures is not a commercial success, but this does not stop the doctor from abandoning his medical practice and concentrating on writing. In 1891 Doyle hits his stride with *A Scandal in Bohemia*, which is an instant best-seller, and Sherlock Holmes quickly becomes the most popular fictional crime solver of all time. The Holmes narratives are early examples of the detective story, a type pioneered by Edgar Allan Poe, and are the first in which logic and scientific knowledge and inquiry are used to solve cases. In Doyle's works, the actual "detective story" often occupies only half of the narrative, the investigation and probing of facts constituting the rest.

Sherlock Holmes's exploits appear in 1891 on a weekly basis in the *Strand Magazine* and are then collected in two volumes, *The Adventures of Sherlock Holmes* and *The Memoirs of Sherlock Holmes*. The tales are narrated by Holmes's loyal colleague, Dr. Watson, who keeps watch over the detective's addictive drug use. In the foreground of nearly all these adventures is Holmes's nemesis, the archvillain Professor Moriarty.

With twenty or so of these stories behind him, Doyle begins to tire of the Holmes character and in 1893 kills him off in *The Final Problem*, which details Moriarty's murder of the detective. The public will have none of this, however, and Doyle is forced to resuscitate his hero. Holmes returns in 1902 in *The Hound of the Baskervilles*, which claims to relate an early case of Holmes's.

During this time Doyle continues to write historical novels. When the Boer War breaks out, he works at a field hospital in Bloemfontein and writes a history of the conflict in an attempt to defend British policy in South Africa. For his efforts he is knighted in 1902.

Queen Victoria does not live to see the fully revived Sherlock Holmes make his reappearance in *The Return of Sherlock Holmes* in 1905, in which it is revealed that Holmes survived his earlier attack. Other stories flow from Sir Arthur's pen until his death in 1930. The ingenious detective lives on and has since achieved cult status among such Holmes devotees as the Baker Street Irregulars and the Speckled Band.

Victoria's long reign was full of notable people who left their mark on the age. Some of them are presented here, gathered around their queen, including Robert Louis Stevenson, Rudyard Kipling, George Bernard Shaw, Joseph Conrad, Thomas Hardy, Charlotte and Emily Brontë, Charles Dickens, James Barrie, Oscar Wilde, Arthur Conan Doyle, William Thackeray, George Eliot (Mary Ann Evans), Edgar Allan Poe (writers); Lewis Carroll (Charles Dodgson: mathematician and writer); William Morris (painter and writer); Thomas Cook (tourist agent); Alfred Tennyson (poet); Alfred Sisley (painter); Ernest Rutherford, Michael Faraday (scientists); Karl Marx (political

philosopher); Daniel O'Connell, William Gladstone, Benjamin Disraeli, Joseph Chamberlain, Richard Cobden, John Russell, Robert Peel, Henry Palmerston (politicians); duke of Wellington (soldier and statesman); Felix Mendelssohn (composer); Florence Nightingale (humanitarian); Charles Darwin (naturalist); Robert Baden-Powell (soldier, founder of Scouting); H. Herbert; Beau Brummell (dandy and wit); Earl Granville, George Cruikshank, Cecil Rhodes, H.A. Oswald, Lord Beaconfield, Lady James Brown Potter, Aubrey Beardsley, Louis of Belgium, Louise of Saxe, Tsar Alexander II, the queen's dog (royal family from a detail from a painting by John Millais).

FAMILY PORTRAIT

Whether through blood ties, marriage, political maneuvering, domestic devotion, or canine loyalty, everyone in this picture was related to Victoria, the grandmother of Europe. As for getting her to smile—that's another story.

Grand Duke Paul of Russia

Princess Philip of Coburg

Louis of Battenberg

Philip of Coburg

Prince Henry of Battenberg

Edward VII

Beatrice, wife of Henry of Battenberg

Alfred of Coburg

Tsar Nicholas II

Alice, grand duchess of Hesse

Kaiser Wilhelm II

Me in 1894

Beatrice of Coburg

My friend John Brown and me

Look how he loves me!

Count Mendsorff
Grand Duke Serge
Princess of Rumania
Prince of Rumania
Louise, duchess of Connaught
Arthur, duke of Connaught
Grand Duke Vladimir
Alfred, duke of Saxe-Coburg-Gotha

Albert and me

Duchess of Connaught
Grand Duchess Vladimir
Duchess of Connaught (another)
Victoria, empress of Germany

Feodora of Saxe-Meiningen
Princess Henry of Russia

Princess Victoria of Battenberg

Princess Alexandra of Coburg

WHICH SIDE

Conservative, Liberal, Liberal,

LIBERAL

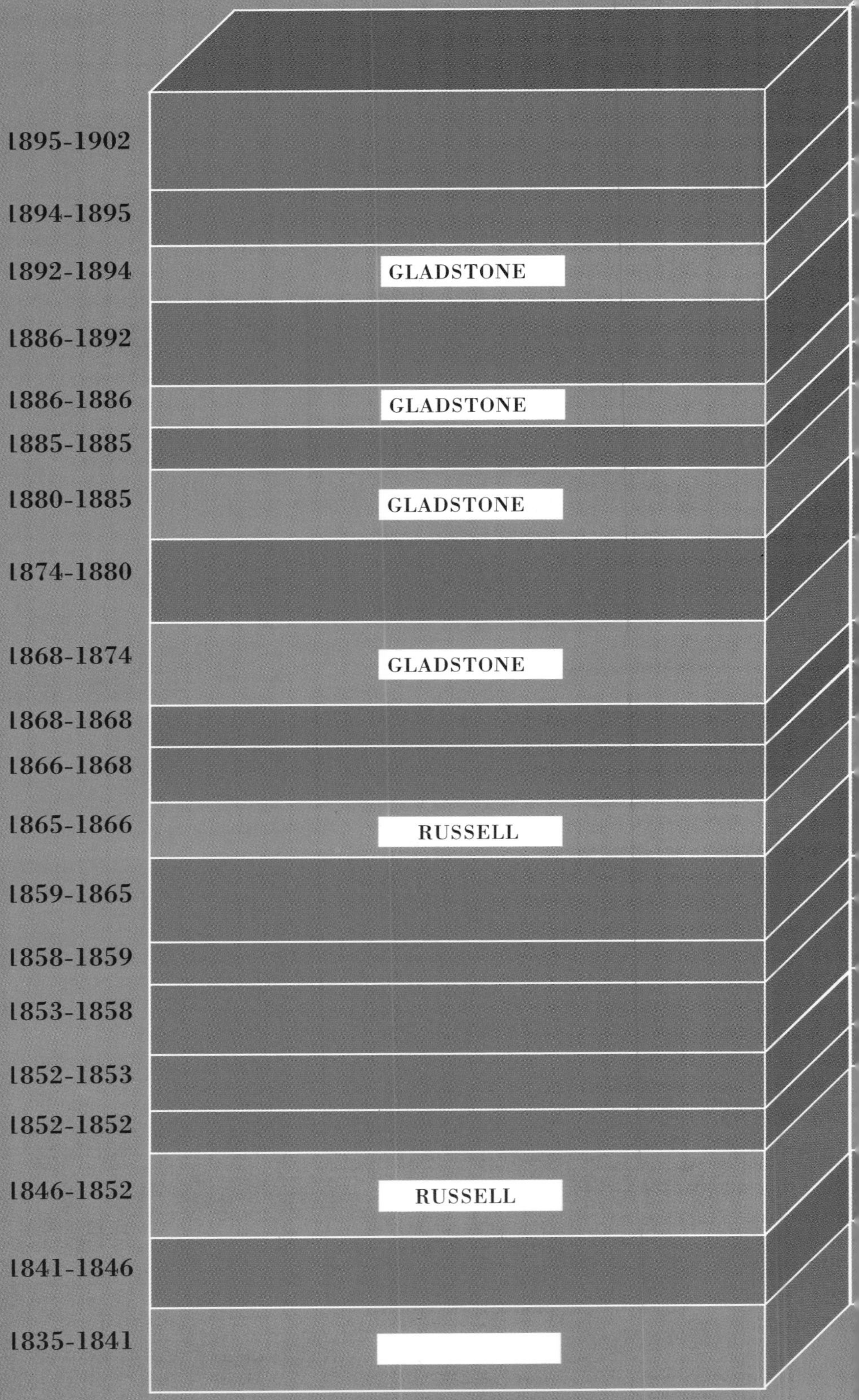
1895-1902
1894-1895
1892-1894
GLADSTONE
1886-1892
1886-1886
GLADSTONE
1885-1885
1880-1885
GLADSTONE
1874-1880
1868-1874
GLADSTONE
1868-1868
1866-1868
1865-1866
RUSSELL
1859-1865
1858-1859
1853-1858
1852-1853
1852-1852
1846-1852
RUSSELL
1841-1846
1835-1841

To the left is the Whig (later Liberal) party, founded around 1680. Under Victoria, the party consisted of radicals, dissatisfied Tory disciples of Robert Peel, and industrialists. They took the name Liberal in the mid nineteenth century.

ARE YOU ON?

Conservative . . .The two parties of British politics

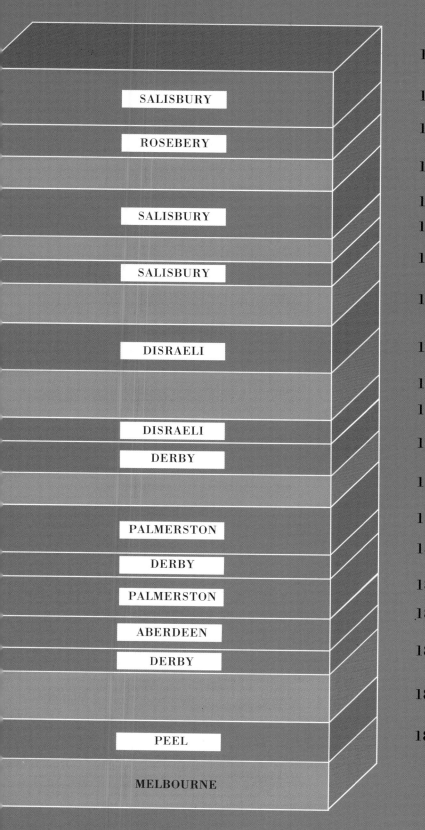

SALISBURY	1895-1902
ROSEBERY	1894-1895
	1892-1894
	1886-1892
SALISBURY	1886-1886
	1885-1885
SALISBURY	1880-1885
	1874-1880
DISRAELI	1868-1874
	1868-1868
	1866-1868
DISRAELI	
DERBY	1865-1866
	1859-1865
PALMERSTON	1858-1859
DERBY	1853-1858
PALMERSTON	1852-1853
ABERDEEN	1852-1852
DERBY	1846-1852
	1841-1846
PEEL	1835-1841
MELBOURNE	

CONSERVATIVE

To the right is the Tory party, which was transformed into the Conservative party in 1832. After the defection of Peel it found its greatest leader in Benjamin Disraeli, who succeeded in strengthening British imperialism and nationalism while managing to gain the support of a large part of the working-class vote.

BRICKS, BRICKS, EVERYWHERE

You can't do much with one brick, but with 12.5 million of them you can build a cathedral. Used during the time of the Stuarts and Tudors, bricks become the building block par excellence after the Great Fire in London in 1666, which destroys nearly all the houses made of wood. In the Victorian age, architects like Augustus Pugin, George Gilbert Scott, and George Edmund Street champion the use of bricks in the medieval building esthetic known as Gothic. They bring about a distinctive revival of that style based on structural clarity, coherence, and functionalism; the neo-Gothic style is to be an organic expression of the moral and spiritual values of the age. All over England buildings of all kinds—from churches to hotels, railway stations, and factories—take on the Gothic look. Westminster Palace, the seat of the Houses of Parliament, is the largest Gothic building in England. Originally built in 1035 as a royal residence, the palace is destroyed by fire in 1053; when a fire in 1834 ravages most of the interior, a competition is held for a new design. Sir Charles Barry is responsible for the Gothic exterior, while Pugin designs the interior. But going back to the story of bricks, Victorian architect John Francis Bentley uses no fewer than 12.5 million of them to build Westminster Cathedral, his neo-Gothic Roman Catholic church in London.

ERROL **FLYNN** OLI DeHAVI

THE **CHARGE** OF THE **LIGHT BRI**

A Warner

"The Crimea was criminal," said Englishman John Bright speaking of the Crimean War, in which the divergent interests of the European powers converged on the Turkish Empire. The war, in which England and France ally with the Turks against Russia, is caused primarily by the decay of the Ottoman Empire and Russia's expansionist ambitions.

The allied army is under the joint command of two very different men: the impetuous English field general Lord Raglan and the cautious French commander Saint-Arnaud.

On October 25, 1854, a tragic event occurs at Balaklava. Because of a poorly worded order by Raglan, which is misunderstood, 673 British cavalrymen charge up a long valley commanded by Russian guns. The guns are overrun, but few of the Light Brigade survive. About half of the men who began the charge are wounded or killed. "It is magnificent, but it isn't war," comments a French eyewitness to this heroic but futile charge.

For the allied forces the Crimean winter of 1854-55 is devastating. Exposure and disease, combined

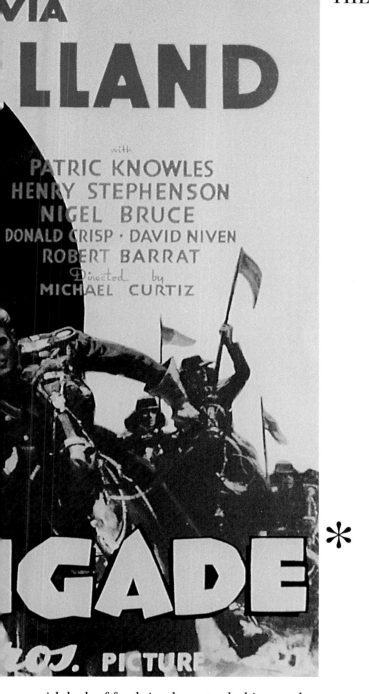

with

PATRIC KNOWLES
HENRY STEPHENSON
NIGEL BRUCE
DONALD CRISP · DAVID NIVEN
ROBERT BARRAT
Directed by
MICHAEL CURTIZ

IGADE

*

OS. PICTURE

FLORENCE NIGHTINGALE
1820-1910

Born to wealth and beauty, Florence Nightingale devotes her life to the care of the sick and suffering. During the Crimean War she organizes a hospital staffed with well-trained nurses, and she applies stringent sanitary regulations that help curb the infectious diseases that the soldiers die from more than their wounds. On her return to England she is received with great pomp at Balmoral by the queen, who gives her a diamond brooch with the inscription "Blessed are the merciful."

In a letter to her, Queen Victoria writes:

"You are, I know, well aware of the high sense I entertain of the Christian devotion which you have displayed during this great and bloody war, and I need hardly repeat to you how warm my admiration is for your services, which are fully equal to those of my dear and brave soldiers, whose sufferings you have had the privilege of alleviating in so merciful a manner."

Florence Nightingale spends the rest of her life writing and working on nursing, hospitals, and the extension of the International Red Cross. She is considered the founder of modern nursing.

with lack of food, inadequate clothing, and insufficient medical supplies, severely hamper their attempts to capture the fortress of Sevastopol; 9,000 men die in the month of February 1855. The allied siege drags on through the bitter winter until the following September, when the bastion is finally taken. The Treaty of Paris in 1856 formally ends the hostilities of a war that really should never have happened.

STEAMING ALONG

From 1815 on, the disciples of George Stephenson, father of the steam engine, waste no time in putting this new form of energy to work in the service of maritime transport. By 1825 the General Steam Navigation Company has fifteen steamships plying the waters between London and various European ports.

In 1838 steamers cross the Atlantic in only nineteen days, a great improvement over the thirty-five days required by sail. This, however, does not mean the end of sailing ships. In fact, they continue to flourish along the trading routes of the empire, from China to Australia and India to Africa.

It takes a clipper about a hundred days to make the journey from China to England. The most famous of these sailing ships is without doubt the *Cutty Sark*, which is built in 1869 in the shipyards of Dumbarton on the Clyde. This splendid 921-ton craft can make the trip between Australia and England at a speed of nineteen knots. The year 1890, however, marks the beginning of the end for these ships, as they are little by little replaced by steamers.

Sail or steam, war or trade, the naval force is one of nineteenth-century England's crowning glories, making it the mistress of the seas for more than sixty years.

LOVE ME, LOVE ME NOT

Of the ten prime ministers who serve Queen Victoria during her sixty-four-year reign—the longest in British history—three stand out as having had a special partnership with her. Lord Melbourne, twice prime minister (1834, 1835-41), teaches the young queen important lessons in statecraft and becomes one of her most trusted confidants. Some thirty years later, two other prime ministers share the spotlight in alternating turns at power: Benjamin Disraeli in 1868, William Gladstone from 1868 to 1873, Disraeli again from 1874 to 1880, Gladstone from 1880 to 1884, then in 1886 and 1892 to 1894. British policy is to crystallize under the impact of these two giants. To the right of Victoria stands Benjamin Disraeli. Of Jewish descent, he is baptized an Anglican Christian at the age of twelve. He is a novelist of distinction. His novels, like himself, are marked by acute wit, liveliness, and immense vigor. To the left of Victoria stands William Gladstone. Born in Liverpool, he attends the best schools in the country, Eton and Oxford. A master of splitting hairs, he is also devoutly religious and has a passion for theological problems, always convincing himself that his ideas are divinely inspired. After many years as a conservative, he turns liberal, and Disraeli, whom he considers the incarnation of evil, is his chief adversary. The queen tries to arbitrate objectively between these two men, but her deep admiration and fondness for Disraeli get the better of her. She is entirely under his spell. Only Disraeli can persuade her to abandon her seclusion and mourning after Albert's death and return to public life, and thanks to him she acquires a zest for life and for her work she never knew existed. From 1868 to 1873 Victoria is not amused. Gladstone is in power again, and the queen passionately dislikes him. She once claims that he addresses her as if she were a "public meeting." Fortunately, Parliament is dissolved in 1874, and the Conservative party wins. The queen welcomes back her beloved Disraeli. How could she not be fond of the person who wrote these words to her on her fifty-sixth birthday: "For today which has given to my country a Sovereign . . . has also given to me, her humble, but chosen servant, a Mistress, whom to serve is to love." In gratitude, the queen elevates her favorite prime minister to the peerage, creating him earl of Beaconsfield. Ever attentive to the queen, Disraeli forces a bill through parliament making her empress of India.

OSCAR

"I have put my genius into my life; all I've put into my works is my talent."
This is how Oscar Fingall O'Flahertie Wills Wilde—known to the world as Oscar Wilde—described himself to his friend the French writer André Gide.

Born in Dublin, Ireland, on October 16, 1854, Wilde was a poet, dramatist, and novelist who captivated his contemporaries with his genius and wit while also attracting a great deal of attention with his extravagant idiosyncrasies. Even well after his death—he died in Paris on November 20, 1900—Wilde continues to exert the same fascination over readers, whether they're introduced to him by way of his only novel, *The Picture of Dorian Gray*, or his plays, such as *Salome*, which was written in French for the actress Sarah Bernhardt.

In his own time, Wilde was not forgiven for flaunting his homosexuality and for exposing—in hilarious detail—all the defects of the society he lived in. Especially in his comedies, he revealed the hypocrisy and duplicity of his contemporaries, who eventually got the better of him by having him sent to prison in 1895 for two years. Whether it is the guilty mother in *Lady Windermere's Fan* or the abandoned mother in *A Woman of No Importance*, Wilde never ceased to unmask the intrigues, the shallowness, the arrogance, and all the wrongs of his times with his characteristic impertinence and wit.

I can resist everything except temptation.

There is only one thing in the world worse than being talked about, and that is not being talked about.

Truth is rarely pure, and never simple.

Experience is the name every one gives to their mistakes.

The old-fashioned respect for the young is fast dying out.

A little sincerity is a dangerous thing, and a great deal of it is absolutely fatal.

A man cannot be too careful in the choice of his enemies.

Please do not shoot the pianist. He is doing his best.

WILDE

*When people agree with me I always feel
that I must be wrong.*

*We are all in the gutter,
but some of us are looking at the stars.*

Bad artists always admire each other's works.

*All women become like their mothers.
That is their tragedy. No man does. That's his.*

*I am the only person in the world
I should like to know thoroughly.*

*In this world there are only two tragedies.
One is not getting what one wants, and the
other is getting it.*

*In married life three is company
and two is none.*

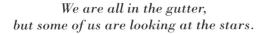

*The only thing that one really knows about human
nature is that it changes.*

There is no sin except stupidity.

Where there is sorrow there is holy ground.

A ROYAL WEBSITE

GERMANY
VICTORIA + ALBERT

Princess Victoria (lst child) + Frederick III, German emperor and king of Prussia

▼

Kaiser Wilhelm II
1859-1941

SPAIN
VICTORIA + ALBERT

Princess Beatrice (9th child) + Henry, prince of Battenberg

▼

King Juan Carlos
b. 1938

GREECE
VICTORIA + ALBERT

Princess Alice (3rd child) + Louis IV, grand duke of Hesse-Darmstadt

▼

Prince Philip of Greece
b. 1921, became duke of Edinburgh when he married
Queen Elizabeth II

NORWAY
VICTORIA + ALBERT

Edward VII (2nd child) + Princess Alexandra, daughter of King
Christian IX of Denmark

▼

King Harold V
b. 1937

ROMANIA
VICTORIA + ALBERT

Alfred (4th child) + Grand Duchess Marie, daughter of Alexander II,
tsar of Russia

▼

King Michael I
b. 1921

RUSSIA
VICTORIA + ALBERT

Alice (3rd child) + Louis IV, grand duke of Hesse-Darmstadt

▼

Princess Alexandra of Hesse-Darmstadt married Nicholas II, tsar of
Russia; the imperial family was assassinated in 1918.

INDIA

The situation in India is among the most pressing problems Victoria faces as queen of England. Since the beginning of the nineteenth century India has been a British possession, and the country is in turmoil because of a series of disastrous events, including the Anglo-Afghan War of 1840, the bloody conquest of Sind in 1843, the Sikh Wars to annex Punjab, and above all the Indian Mutiny of 1857, a major revolt by the sepoys (Indian troops) against British rule. This mutiny has serious effects on relations between the two countries, and England, which has sought to be a source of enlightenment in

India, now chooses not to intervene in areas that touch on religion and local custom. Economically, the British East India Company no longer has a monopoly on business after the revision of its charter in 1833. India is now open to private enterprise and depends on what it can get from other countries, namely England, a situation that gives birth to capitalism in India. The Indian Mutiny

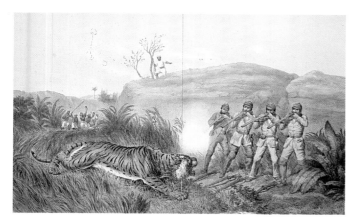

effectively ends the control of India by the East
India Company and transfers it directly to the
British crown. The English governor general
becomes the viceroy of India, and the country for
the most part comes under crown rule, while the
hundreds of autonomous states that are
protectorates of the crown are governed by
maharajas.

On January 1, 1876, Queen Victoria is
proclaimed empress of India. Though she never sets
foot in the country that is the "chief jewel in the
imperial crown," Victoria contributes to local
folklore by having two Hindu servants at her beck
and call.

Victoria declares that the British presence in
India is "indispensable to national prosperity" and
that "the Indians must know that no one has the
right to dislike their dark skin and that the greatest
wish of their empress is to see them happy and
prosperous."

*the church, the music, etc., and everything connected with the
wedding day until he bids his daughter goodbye when she leaves for
the honeymoon.*

ON HORSEBACK

*Noteworthy changes have occurred these last years in the area of
equestrian fashion. Black jackets are passé. Rather one recommends
a golfing outfit with a Norfolk jacket and a bowler. Straw hats are
no longer advised. It is extremely impolite to make noise while
galloping or to pass a lady even if it is to prevent her from losing her
balance. Riders must keep to their left, pedestrians to their right. In
seeing a lady to her carriage, a gentleman offers his right arm to her
and opens the door with the left hand. He shelters her
from the rain with his umbrella. If he is to travel
with her, he takes the seat which faces the
opposite direction in which they are going
and he gives the coachman the orders. He
does not open the window unless a lady
has asked him to do so. It is to be noted
that the word brougham is
pronounced as "broom"
in one syllable. This
might seem a trifle,
but it is such
details that are the
mark of belonging
to good English
society.*

BICYCLING

*The etiquette of bicycling seems simple enough, especially to
those who are familiar with the rule of the road in riding or
driving. But thousands of bicyclists belong to a class which is
ignorant of the charms of horse exercise. . . . Not very long ago a
woman on a bicycle . . . caused a terrible accident in which a coach
was overturned . . . and a couple of valuable horses so badly
damaged that they had to be shot.*

VISITING CARDS

*It used to be the rule that so long as a girl was unmarried and
lived at home, even when she might have reached the indefinite
age of "spinsterhood," she had no separate visiting card, but
shared that of her mother, under whose name her own appeared.
But now the old rule has become pretty obsolete. . . . The card
must be a thin white piece of pasteboard, absolutely plain,
without borders or ornament of any kind. The name occupies
the center, and is always in copperplate italic characters.*

WEDDINGS

*Servants go nearly wild with excitement when there is a
wedding going on. They are so anxious to be of use in every
way that they incline to neglect their own special department.
With reference to the choice of horses . . . at one time a pair of grays
were considered indispensable for the bride's carriage, but that has
all changed, and it is thought better taste to have browns or bays.
The fact is that a smart pair of grays has been found to attract
much notice, with the consequence that an undesirable crowd
frequently assembles at the bride's house . . . Crying is no longer
fashionable. It has followed fainting into
the moonlight land of half-forgotten
things. It used to be in the program
of weddings that brides should weep
in the vestry at least when signing
their maiden name for the last time . . .
She may shed a furtive tear or two at
parting from the "dearest old dad in the
world," or "darling mums." . . . The
bridegroom has to give all the
bridesmaids a present, as well as their
bouquets. The father pays for the floral decorations of*

DO WHAT?

Humphry's books of manners (one volume for men, another for women).
she says about:

TEA

Gentlemen of quality are highly sought after for five o'clock tea parties. Precise tasks are assigned to them. They must pass the teacups, sugar, milk, cakes, and scones while carrying on an intelligent and witty conversation with the ladies. They must get up each time a lady enters the drawing room or leaves it and, if possible, open the door. If the gentleman is witty and amuses his listeners, the ladies must be careful of the manner in which they laugh. There is nothing more vulgar than the "ha ha" of the ill-mannered. The proper laugh must be crystal-clear and musical. The great French actress Sarah Bernhardt, with her golden voice, has undoubtedly an incomparable silvery laugh. Doctors now assure us that laughing is a marvelous therapy for the spleen, as it stimulates the blood and promotes digestion. And why deprive oneself of it provided that it be truly elegant.

BALLS

Only thirty or forty years ago there were great houses with many servants where one could very easily entertain and organize large soirees and balls. Alas, times have changed. Houses are now smaller and staffed by fewer servants. It is sometimes even necessary to rent large rooms in hotels because one can no longer receive at home. Such is life. At a ball, there are, unfortunately, those badly brought-up young men who ask the prettiest young ladies to dance first while ignoring those less endowed. This behavior is obviously not to be tolerated. Young men of good society are quickly recognized as those who ask the "wallflowers" to dance first. It may happen that while waltzing, for example, a couple falls. It is only proper, then, that the gentleman excuse himself to his partner and to the lady of the house. When the dance is over, the gentleman bows and thanks his partner.

TRAVELING DRESS

Traveling costumes consist of tweed, serge, Irish frieze, homespun, and other all-wool materials, and are of the class of tailor-mades. In hot weather white muslins, piqués, and flowered or pale muslins are worn by the sea, with openwork white stockings and white shoes. Alpacas, surahs, foulards, and mohairs are suitable for seaside and traveling dress. To wear satin, brocade, or rich heavy silks is as great a solecism as for a man to don frock coat and silk hat at seaside places or when traveling. . . . Evening dress includes two styles, full and demi-toilette. The former exacts uncovered arms and shoulders; the latter admits of partially covering both . . . The princess of Wales and her daughters favor a less decolleté style.

THE ENGAGED GIRL

The bride-elect usually visits her future husband's family shortly after her engagement. This is often a rather trying time, for she knows she is the object of very critical examination on the part of her prospective mother-in-law and her sisters-in-law, to say nothing of father-in-law and brothers-in-law. Many an intended marriage has been broken off after the fiancée's visit. Mothers have an idea that no girl is good enough for their sons . . . Consequently all is not roses during such visits. A gentle, lovable girl, however, frequently wins golden opinions on such occasions, especially if she be of the unselfish sort, and does not wholly monopolize the time and attention of the son of the house.

DINNERS

When an invitation is for a precise hour, eight o'clock, for example, one must be punctual and no more than five minutes late, which would be the height of impoliteness. On entering the drawing room the gentleman must, no matter what, first greet the hostess wherever she may be, even if he recognizes someone he knows near the door. He then shakes the hands of those he knows and waits to be introduced to the others by the hostess. At table, he converses about everything except the weather. . . . The spoon is for the soup, the fish knife and fork are placed on the outside as this dish follows the soup. It is not good manners to thank the servants each time they serve you. It is preferable not to drink too much wine and to make as little noise as possible with the silver. Bread is broken by hand and not with the knife. Be careful of soup on the mustache. Curry dishes are eaten with fork and spoon. It is quite passé to wait until the others have been served to begin. When it is time for the liqueurs and someone offers you Chartreuse or Benedictine, above all do not answer "Both."

THE VICTORIA

History may never forget the excitement of the glittering days in June 1897 when all of England celebrates the Diamond Jubilee of Queen Victoria—sixty years of uninterrupted reign, the longest in the history of the country. On June 22 the queen, surrounded by members of her family, crowned heads, and representatives from all over the British Empire, rides through London in ceremonial carriages to the tumultuous acclaim of the people. Leaving Buckingham Palace the royal procession makes its way to St. Paul's Cathedral for a thanksgiving service. Afterward, on her way back to Buckingham Palace, the queen crosses London Bridge and goes through the poor areas of the city south of the Thames. From the palace the queen, then seventy-eight years old, telegraphs a jubilee message to her subjects around the world: "From my heart I thank my beloved people. May God bless them!" The festivities last two weeks: among the events is a garden party at Buckingham, a parade of colonial troops at Windsor, and a reception for the colonial prime ministers and 180 Protestant prelates from the English-speaking countries of the realm. But the climax of the festivities is the naval show at Spithead on June 26, presided over by the prince of Wales, in which 173 ships bring home the splendor of the British Empire's heritage in a display of pomp and power.

JUBILEE

⑤ : *How do you explain the famous Industrial Revolution, which seems to be one of the hallmarks of your reign?*
QUEEN V: Let us first remind you that the Industrial Revolution hardly leapt into being, but had been coming for a long time, driven on by developments in the preceding century. We had our so-called turnpike trusts, those private companies that improved roads and such, and they built quality tollways with our famous macadamized surfaces. In the mid-eighteenth century the country was positively crisscrossed by canals, and in our reign, of course, it was the railroad. Thanks to George Stephenson's potent steam locomotive, our railways proliferated and created an economic revolution. By the middle of our century about 5,000 miles of railway stretched across the U.K.—United Kingdom, to you. Railways quickened all aspects of our economy, more coal to be dug up, more iron to be made—we've never understood personally just how that's done—and many people gainfully employed all day long. And they provided cheaper and faster transportation of our goods throughout the country, and ultimately the world.

⑤ : *Yes. But what goods are you referring to?*
QUEEN V: Oh, we'd say textiles, for instance. They remain our primary industrial sector. Not only wool from our

TO KNOW

homebred sheep, but also cotton imported from India and the West Indies. Also let us not forget the silk and Indian jute woven in Scotland that we are beginning to export. As for our other industrial sectors, coal is our most used energy source. Dig it up! At the beginning of the eighteenth century we produced 3 million tons of coal, and now we are at nearly 25 million!

🌀 : *You were proclaimed empress of India in 1876. Your jubilees in 1887 and 1897 celebrated imperial England, or, should we say, imperialist England. Looking back now, can you explain the rationale behind your foreign policy?*

QUEEN V: We need hardly justify the "splendid isolation" of our island nation. We realize that we have been reproached for having chosen the path of adventure over responsibilities in Europe. But the truth is we have served our country's best interests by extending British rule to the four corners of the world. Our colonies are of basically two types. The first, colonies of permanent white settlers that can grow in wealth and population until they form new nations. Canada has been a dominion since 1867, and there are the examples of Australia, New Zealand, and South Africa, where, alas, we are still having difficulties.

The other type of colony serves trading purposes. One kind of colony provides us with raw materials. We are thinking of India, for example. The other consists of commercial centers, naval bases, or strategic points from which our trade can be controlled and protected, and these areas are a source of pride and prestige for us. We have carved out advantageous areas in China consisting of five major ports: Canton, Shanghai, Hong Kong— and we forget the others, but they're glorious. On the China route we control Singapore, which we founded in 1819.

🌀 : *Can Your Majesty tell us in a few sentences what she would like to be remembered for in her sixty years or so of domestic policy?*

QUEEN V: Young man, how can you expect us to summarize in a few phrases that which has preoccupied us for our entire life as well as those of the ten prime ministers who served us? Nevertheless, we shall plunge ahead. Undoubtedly, we had our share of troubles. When our head was crowned in 1837, we found a country where everything was difficult, there was suffering among the people, among the children and the less privileged. They wanted to rise from their misery, and

sometimes they resorted to violence. We do not entirely blame them for this, and we have tried—with the invaluable help of our beloved Albert—to do everything we could to help them.

Where are we today? Misery has diminished. Women and children now have a more decent life thanks to laws regulating working hours. We have gone from an agricultural nation to an industrial nation, from an essentially rural population to an urban one, and from a nation of agricultural workers to one of factory workers. As for the landed gentry, they have become businessmen and engineers. We have built schools, hospitals, sewage systems, and have undertaken projects to build housing. Steam and electrical power have dramatically changed our daily lives. Yes, we believe we have contributed to changing the lives of our people. We are now a country of progress.

🌀 : *One last question, Your Highness. Can you tell us, please, how many princes it takes to screw in a light bulb?*

QUEEN V: We've heard that one before, young man, and we were not amused.

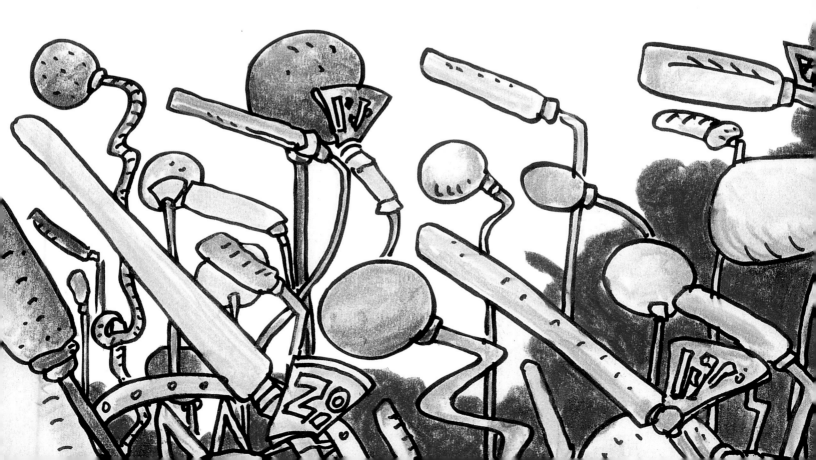

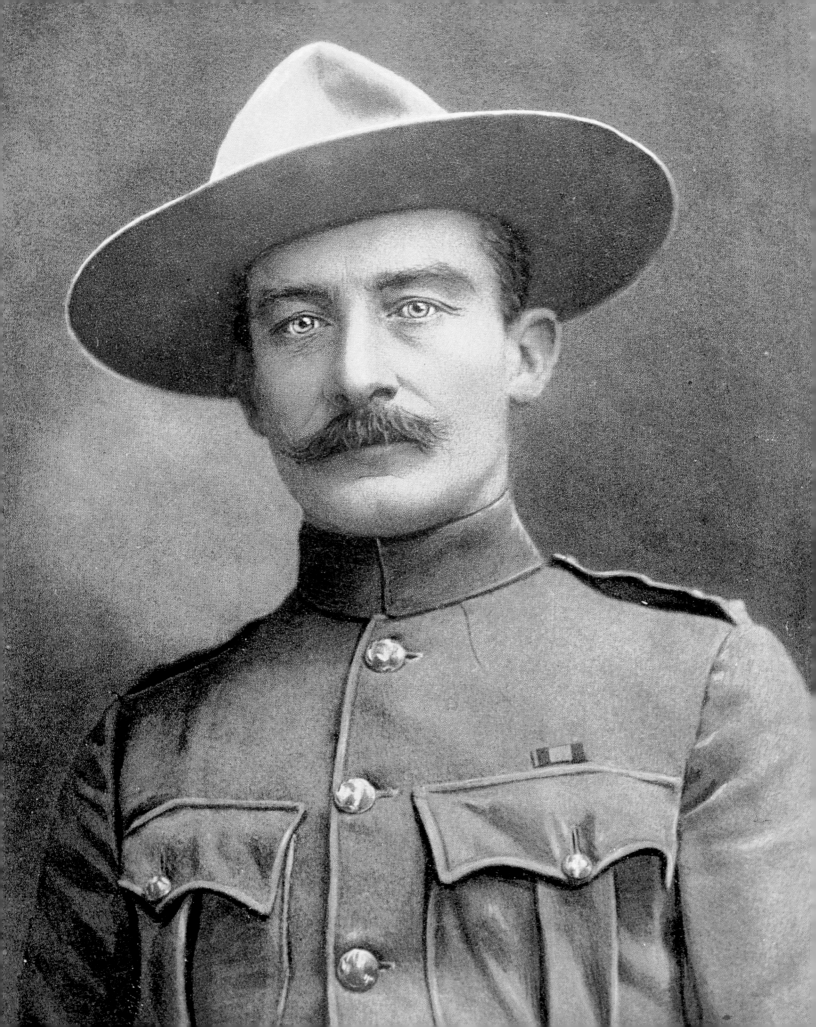

BE PREPARED!

It is 1900, near the start of the Boer War. In order to save the town of Mafeking, which has neither arms nor fortifications to defend itself, Colonel Robert Baden-Powell calls on every resource he can muster. He mobilizes all the young boys of the town and turns them into scouts, spies, and liaison officers. These courageous boys do a fine job and prove instrumental in holding the town through a 211-day siege. Years later, Baden-Powell, yearning for the idealism of his boys—which he finds so lacking in the youth of his day—decides to organize the boy scout movement. The rest is history. This anecdote is not meant to deny the true tragedy of the Boer War. In one week—aptly called "Black Week"—three English generals are defeated in a row: Gatacre at Stormberg on December 10, 1899, Methuen at Magersfontein on the eleventh, and Buller at Colenso on the fifteenth. The British hardly know what has hit them. How can a motley gang of undisciplined farmers defeat the mighty troops of the British Empire? The Dutch settlers, or Boers—derived from a Dutch word for farmer or peasant—are not so disorganized as the English think. They can field an army 45,000 strong and have a hundred cannon. The English have a force of only 27,000 men, and these are scattered all over South Africa. The conflict between the Boers and the English colonists in the southern part of Africa has been simmering for a long time. In 1877 the British government annexes the Boer republic of Transvaal. The Boers revolt in 1881 and regain self-rule, although the republic stays nominally under British control.

Baden-Powell

The discovery of gold in 1886 in the Rand region of Transvaal leads to a great influx of Uitlanders, or foreigners, most of them British. The Boers aren't going to put up with the situation; they're poised for war. A string of Boer victories over British troops in 1899 shocks the English nation. But Victoria proclaims, "We are not interested in the possibilities of defeat. They do not exist," and Britain rushes her two most famous generals, Lord Kitchener and General Frederick Sleigh Roberts, to take command of the largest British army ever assembled, with Canada, Australia, and New Zealand providing reinforcements that swell the troops to more than 250,000 men. Slowly the tide of battle turns. Before the end of 1900 the Boer states of Transvaal and the Orange Free State are invaded and their armies defeated. But the Boers refuse to surrender and for eighteen months mobile commando units—the word *commando* comes from the Afrikaans word *kommando*, a detachment of Boer troops—wage guerrilla war. The Treaty of Vereeniging, signed on May 31, 1902, finally ends hostilities. The complacency of Victorian England has been shaken by the Boer War. From disaster, defeat, and final triumph Britain learns an important lesson: isolation can be perilous as well as splendid, and even the greatest empire on earth can crumble if it stands alone without allies and friends in times of danger. Shortly after, Britain ends its splendid isolation by concluding an alliance with Japan in 1902 and by declaring an "understanding" with France in 1904 over the many colonial disputes that divided them.

Windsor Castle.
Feb: 19. 1874

The Queen has just seen Mr Gladstone who has tendered his resignation & that of his colleagues, which the Queen has accepted. Therefore

HANDWRITING ANALYSIS

This handwriting is plainly that of an extrovert: large, ample, buoyant, slanting forward and extending full range from top to bottom, with broad capital letters and T's crossed long and straight; in short, a nimble hand on paper.

It is the writing of a woman who thrives in society, who thinks and acts according to the conventions of her world, who affirms the opinions of her time, and who keeps those who don't agree with her at a distance. This apparent adaptability, though, often masks an uneasiness within, a deep-seated fear of loss. It is likely that an impersonal and repressive education was responsible for squashing any affective impulses the young child may have had, leaving her scarred forever. When she was growing up, she had to keep quiet and hide who she really was, and it was this life held in secret that most likely hardened her.

The handwriting we see indicates that how she feels plays a major part in the way she makes her decisions and how she behaves in every arena of her life.

The queen needs to be in a climate of harmony; she needs human warmth; she needs to feel wanted. She can be won over with a gentle touch. When confident, she can be impassioned, serious, and affectionate. She wants to be at the center of the action and shields herself by being partial. She never betrays herself; she never loses her self-control; she is exacting. Except for a chosen few, the well-being of others is not of great concern to her, and she can, in fact, be completely indifferent to them. She will not tolerate anyone meddling in her affairs, and she wants to be all-powerful. All the signs of willfulness are there: the writing is strong, unyielding, even relentless, and points to an indomitable spirit that is as steadfast as an anchor. The writing is also tangled in places, indicating that she can get carried away with her emotions, whether it is jealousy, joy, or tenderness. As far as her intelligence is concerned, she can confuse what is important for what is unimportant. She does not think logically, and she often lacks subtlety. She is not an intellectual; she is most likely not even interested in the matters of the mind. Jealous of her prerogatives, she will not stand for anyone who contradicts her. She can express herself inaccurately at times and claim that she is being "objective." She is convinced that she is right—probably in reaction to a childhood in which everyone sought to prove her wrong.

WHAT COLOR IS MY

CHART OF THE WORLD
SHOWING BRITISH EMPIRE
1901.

Submarine Telegraph Cables thus Sub.Tel
Arrows indicate the directions of the Ocean Currents
Distances on the Steam boat routes are given in Eng. Miles

* THE BRITISH EMPIRE IN 1897

EMPIRE*?

EUROPE
Great Britain, Ireland, Cyprus, Gibraltar, Channel Islands, Malta
Surface area: 157,500 square miles
Population: 43,210,000

AFRICA
Ashanti, Basutoland, Bechuanaland, British East Africa, British Somaliland, Cape Colony, Egypt, Gambia, Gold Coast, Natal, Nigeria, Northern Rhodesia, Nyasaland, Sierra Leone, Southern Rhodesia, Swaziland, Transvaal, Uganda
Surface area: 2,150,000 square miles
Population: 37,900,000

AMERICAS
Antigua, Bahamas, Barbados, Bermuda, British Guiana, British Honduras, British Virgin Islands, Canada, Grand Cayman, Grenada, Jamaica, Montserrat, Nevis, Newfoundland, St. Christopher, St. Lucia, St. Vincent, Tobago, Trinidad
Surface area: 3,094,000 square miles
Population: 6,898,000

ASIA
Aden, Brunei, Ceylon, Hong Kong, India, Labuan, Malay Federated States, North Borneo, Papua New Guinea, Sarawak, Singapore
Surface area: 1,700,000 square miles
Population: 296,500,000

AUSTRALIA
New South Wales, New Zealand, Northern Territory, Queensland, South Australia, Tasmania, Victoria, Western Australia
Surface area: 3,100,000 square miles
Population: 4,000,000

ATLANTIC OCEAN
Ascension, Falkland Islands, Gough, St. Helena, Sandwich Islands, Tristan da Cunha
Surface area: 8,670 square miles
Population: 6,200

INDIAN OCEAN
Amirante, Andaman, Chagos, Christmas, Keeling, Kuria Muria, Laccodive, Maldives, Mauritius, Seychelles, Socotra, Zanzibar
Surface area: 1,200 square miles
Population: 400,000

PACIFIC OCEAN
Antipodes, Bounty, Campbell, Chatham, Ellice, Fiji, Gilbert, Kermadec, Lord Howe, Norfolk, Pitcairn, Solomon
Surface area: 7,500 square miles
Population: 150,000

GRAND TOTAL
Surface area: 10,218,870 square miles
Population: 389,064,200

The year 1900 is the beginning of the end. The Boer War, a bitter winter, failing eyesight, the loss of dear ones, all these trials weigh heavily on the poor queen. On December 12, she makes her last public appearance at Windsor Castle. Two days later she commemorates the thirty-ninth anniversary of the death of her beloved Albert. On December 18 the queen leaves for Osborne House in the Scottish Highlands, and the world soon learns that her health is visibly affected by worry over the Boer War. She suffers "intensely" as the casualty list mounts and begins to look drawn and anxious. She starts to lose her memory, which has always served her so well. She becomes irritable whenever a word or name escapes her. She is shattered to learn on Christmas Day that her old friend Lady Churchill has died. The opening entry in Victoria's journal for 1901 reads: "Another year begun and I am feeling so weak and unwell that I enter upon it sadly." On January 12 she has a twenty-minute discussion with Colonial Secretary Joseph Chamberlain about the war. On the fifteenth the queen goes out for a drive. It is the last time she will leave the house alive. Her doctors have given up all hope. The queen's condition has been degenerating for the last six months. On the nineteenth she can no longer speak. She dies, surrounded by her children and grandchildren, on January 22 at 6:30 P.M. She is eighty-one years old.

The queen leaves specific instructions for her funeral. The service is to be at St. George's Chapel at Windsor; it is to be in the day and not at night, as had been traditional; there is to be a minimum of ceremony. The funeral must be white, she instructs, as on the day of her wedding, which she says was the happiest day of her life. For forty years the widow of Windsor has rarely been seen in anything other than black; now that she hopes to be reunited with Albert the time for mourning is over. She is dressed in white silk with a white widow's cap and veil. The objects she wants buried with her include Albert's dressing gown, a plaster cast of his hand, family photographs, jewelry, and bouquets of lily-of-the-valley, her favorite flower.

On February 1 the queen's coffin is placed on the quarterdeck of the royal yacht *Albert* and begins its journey to London. It is followed by Victoria's son King Edward VII on board the *Victoria and Albert*, and her grandson Kaiser Wilhelm II in his imperial yacht. Throughout the journey from Cowes to Portsmouth, fleets of warships from many nations thunder their salute; to the east lies the mighty battleship *Hatsuse*, a tribute from the Japanese mikado. The next morning, the coffin is taken by train to Victoria Station in London; all along the journey people can been seen kneeling reverently on the ground as the queen passes. For the first time in modern history, London is able to take part in a sovereign's funeral. The streets are decorated in purple and white as she wanted. Her coffin is carried on a simple gun carriage.

On February 4 she is buried in the mausoleum at Frogmore near Windsor Castle. Above the door of the royal shrine are the words: "His mourning widow, Victoria the Queen, directed that all that is mortal of Prince Albert be placed in this sepulcher. A.D. 1862. Farewell, beloved! Here, at last, will I rest with thee; with thee in Christ I will rise again." For Victoria, the promised day has come.